SOUL SEARCHING

TO PTSD HELL AND BACK TWICE

DONNA SIGGERS

Foreword by Jim Fletcher

Also, by Donna Siggers

THE WARWICK COOPER THRILLERS

Broken

Betrayal

Bound

THE BLANDFORD THRILLERS

Faces of the Missing

GETTING YOUR LIFE BACK

LOST SOUL: Broken Soul to Soul on Fire

SOUL SEARCHING: To PTSD Hell and Back Twice

HEAL YOUR MIND

FREE SPIRIT: How to Break Beyond Limitations

Copyright © (2022) Donna Siggers

ISBN: 979-8868429866

Published by DS Books.

The moral right of Donna Siggers to be identified as the author of this work has been asserted in accordance with the Copyright, Designs and Patents Act of 1988.

All rights reserved. No part of this publication may be reproduced, stored in a retrieval system, or transmitted in any form by any means, electronically, mechanical, photocopying, recording or otherwise, without the prior permission of the copyright owner of this book.

Cover designed by Donna Siggers.

For Levi Perry

You are beautiful, a lady I'm proud to call my friend, a warrior in your own right. I'm blessed to have you in my life.

"She was powerful, not because she wasn't scared but because she went on so strongly, despite the fear."

Atticus

Just because you fail once, doesn't mean you're gonna fail at everything. Keep trying, hold on and always, always, always believe in yourself. Because if you don't, then who will, sweetie.

Marilyn Monroe

Contents

Contents 7

Acknowledgement 11

Foreword 15

Preface 18

Masks 27

CHAPTER ONE 28

Trauma 28

CHAPTER TWO 29

Childhood Views 29

CHAPTER THREE 31

Amnesia 31

CHAPTER FOUR 32

Sporty Days 32

CHAPTER FIVE 36

Relationships 36

CHAPTER SIX 40

Trauma Bonding 40

CHAPTER SEVEN 42

Looking Over My Shoulder 42

CHAPTER EIGHT 45

AT THE SCENE 45

CHAPTER NINE 47

ILLNESS 47

FROM CHAOS 59

CHAPTER TEN 60

SELF-REFLECTION 60

MEMORIES 67

CHAPTER ELEVEN 68

MY RELATIONSHIP WITH THERAPY 68

CHAPTER TWELVE 73

KITCHEN EXTENSIONS (...FROM KITCHEN SAGAS) 73

CHAPTER THIRTEEN 77

THE SCIENCE: BRAIN RESPONSE TO TRAUMA & PAIN 77

CHAPTER FOURTEEN 78

MY PERSONAL PAIN 78

PAIN 83

CHAPTER FIFTEEN 84

STRESS HORMONES 84

CHAPTER SIXTEEN 86

PAIN SIGNALS 86

CHAPTER SEVENTEEN 88

LINKING STRESS AND PAIN 88

CHAPTER EIGHTEEN 92

INFLAMMATION 92

CHAPTER NINETEEN 94
Immediate Hormone Response in the Brain 94

CHAPTER TWENTY 96
Stress and Inflammation 96

CHAPTER TWENTY-ONE 99
Limbic system 99

CHAPTER TWENTY-TWO 104
Substance P 104

CHAPTER TWENTY-THREE 106
Loneliness 106

CHAPTER TWENTY-FOUR 109
Living with Anxiety & Flashbacks 109
Transparency 116

CHAPTER TWENTY-FIVE 117
Nightmares 117

CHAPTER TWENTY-SIX 120
Adrenaline and Me 120

CHAPTER TWENTY-SEVEN 125
Dealing with Fear 125
Empathy 129

CHAPTER TWENTY-EIGHT 130
Hyper-me 130

CHAPTER TWENTY-NINE 132

Stormy Nights 132

Epilepsy 135

CHAPTER THIRTY 137

Building A Memory 137

CHAPTER THIRTY-ONE 154

Returning to Hell 154

Depression 158

CHAPTER THIRTY-TWO 159

Dissociation and Reliving 159

CHAPTER THIRTY-THREE 167

Cycle of Doom 167

CHAPTER THIRTY-FOUR 171

Remembering in Order to Heal 171

CHAPTER THIRTY-FIVE 174

Living Free 174

CHAPTER THIRTY-SIX 176

Final Word 176

Freedom 183

About the Author 184

Acknowledgement

Geographical distance is no barrier for love or bonds shared between a mother and her children. To each of you my unconditional love and support, always. There could never be enough thanks or gratitude I could convey for the support you've all provided me. Now, it truly is my turn to step up once more, having taken back control of my life. As much as I'd have liked to hold back my secrets forever, they ate away at me. Forming a huge part of my trauma, letting go was the only way to heal totally. That my life is so public must be unbearably difficult and for that I'm sorry. That our relationships hold no hierarchy in the way "normal" parent/child relationships might is testament to how you all stepped up in my time of need while you were all still so young. To be each of your equal is an honour. I cannot convey how much love I have for you all.

Lockdown was harsh, keeping all of us apart, and despite only being a short distance away from my parents at that time it certainly took a toll. That I've now moved away is now our harsh reality. Mum and dad, I promise to visit regularly. Thank you for all you have done in support of my recovery and, of course, throughout life. Love you always.

Watching me battle PTSD wasn't quite the experience Dave expected but that's the one he had to get to grips with quickly if he were to continue to be part of my life. Thank you darling for the nightly brews at three(ish) in the morning, as you learnt the hard way to cope with what I was going through. It was a long nine months, I know. A million apologies for the intrusion of your sleep, although ironic that I slept better back then, than I do now. Darling, I love you more than words could convey.

Levi Perry, you rock my beautiful warrior friend. I dedicated this book to you because I want you to know how much our special friendship means to me. Without you knowing at the time, you held my head above water the nine months I was away from social media. You kept my adverts going and checked up on me. I'd made this decision before we'd actually met, that's how special a person you are. To share that long awaited hug was priceless. To hear you sing live, gold dust. Hearing you sing "Warrior" in person was especially special for me, a moment that made the hairs on the back of my neck stand to attention. You have the most beautiful heart and soul and please know that I love you. As we always say… hugs x

Jim Fletcher, you are as good as family as you well know. What people might not realise is that we met on Twitter but over the years, I've got to know your whole family and that you've been there for me since twenty-eighteen, when you launched LondonCrime. To have championed me through achievements both personal and book related, and to know you're there during the darker times too, and that you understand why I go quiet and notice when I'm missing from social media, makes me appreciate our friendship even more. The times we go missing simultaneously so neither of us are aware are the worrying times. That you went on to trust me with what was originally a small team (that's now grown) to support you with your website was a huge lift for me. We've all met and made life-long friends through what you begun and what we do. Thank you from the bottom of my heart for stepping up and writing the foreword for Soul Searching. Your words made my eyes leak when I first read them for, they encompass our brother/sister relationship that we've built over time.

Generally speaking, I don't send my books out to ARC readers. Given the content and subject matter of this book I invited friends I trusted for a preview read friends who I knew would both understand and put me in my place if they thought I'd taken matters too far! Thank you to each of you that, firstly I trust enough to undertake this task and secondly to those of you that came back with ways for me to improve the content. Jim Fletcher and Jeannie Chambers, both of you gave me the confidence to write two new 'deep' chapters that I believe give richer explanations as to why 'matters' occur. My deepest gratitude to you both.

Three groups deserving of recognition, for however tough it gets I still participate are those belonging to Lizzie Chantree and Christopher Moss—both are talented authors and lovely people. Both groups provide support differently for writers and readers within them. The third is a group for those of us suffering brain injuries and is packed with fun. I'm not naming names because we're a little undercover—I've made some amazing buddies who understand in this group, and this is the place I go to 'escape' for it's a blast. From the bottom of my heart—thank you to you all.

As a final message I'd like to turn a couple of tables around and thank some folk who, without their presence in my life it wouldn't be quite the same. They are the ones who, at the end of the day, give this book authenticity.

This is owning my life, by the way!

Firstly, to the two people who have stalked / do stalk me (despite it really not being okay) thank you. Those who know me well will realise how diligently I fought against it before, and that however gruelling it gets, I won't be beaten into submission. Anyone wishing to place me into a position in which they'd like me to feel 'victimised' would do well to realise I've the backbone of an army, the knowledge required to win their game, but moreover the courage to stand tall and speak out. The word 'victim' by the way does not enter my vocabulary for I am a survivor, and anyone would do well to remember that.

Secondly, to my old boss, thanks for your incompetence, without which I'd not know the wonderful people in my life with which I've now been blessed. Not only is my social media filled with truly talented and creative individuals, and amazing people who have turned their lives around, but to top it these people have become wonderful friends. Social media, for me, isn't a place just for online interaction—we get out there and meet up in person too. As a result of head trauma, I have met the man I want to spend the rest of my life with, and we did that through mutual interests and mutual friends. When it comes to turning a negative into a massive positive, I am the lady to do so. That makes the life of hell I face more than worth it!

Foreword

There has always been a kind of "stigma" to mental health. All of my life, I never really "understood" people who claimed to have mental health issues. It just wasn't in my vocabulary. I am guilty as charged of being ignorant to something that I had no personal experience of, that is, until my own mind broke in 2018!

You don't see it coming, it doesn't necessarily give you any warning signs (at least, not that you'd notice). You may have been dealing with one thing after another, sad things, or stressful things. You think you are coping, but your mood changes, people start to notice that you seem "different" (or no one notices).

An accumulation of events in my own life (for which I won't divulge here) led to me being sent home from my workplace by the occupational health nurse. I got home, and then it hit! I was a wreck that could barely string a sentence together. I struggled with talking to anyone, and preferred my own company as I didn't want to mix with anyone in the real world.

It was during my own mental breakdown that I commenced to rebuild my mind and try to get some kind of "normality" back into my life. I needed something that didn't "belong" to anyone else other than me. Something that I could focus on, as while I was focused on building my website, no other feelings could enter my mind. Londoncrime was born and dedicated to my late dad who passed away on Christmas day 2014. Not long after launching my website, Donna Siggers reached out to me asking questions on web design, promotion, and all sorts of other stuff that many would find quite boring! She already knew all this stuff as she had done it all before, but this is where I started to know more about Donna's memory loss issues, and I was simply reminding her how to do things. With many shared interests (especially crime and its history) a lasting friendship followed, we help each other out with a wide range of things, and I cannot thank Donna enough for her excellent help and advice through some very difficult times (achieving more than my own counsellor)! It is truly an honour to be contributing to this book!

I have followed Donna's journey over the last few years and have been witness to some of the many challenges faced, some of which would make most people extremely nervous. Travelling from her home to the USA to be awarded the "Thriller" category winner at the Author Academy awards for her thriller "Broken," would have been absolutely terrifying. With anxiety levels through the roof, leaving home to catch trains, then to take flights, land in unknown territory, and locate the event. I was providing as much support and encouragement from the moment Donna received the invite, right through the journey, to picking up the prize and talking to a large crowd, and then the journey home. Each and every step was a challenge and achievement that speaks volumes for her determination and courage to overcome any obstacles in her path. I'm not sure who was struggling to comprehend the enormity of the event, me, or Donna!

Donna understands how the mind works. Not necessarily just through extensive studying, but through lived experiences, trauma, and

PTSD. This revealing book will certainly open your eyes not only to her life and challenges, but to better understanding of mental health issues and the many forms it can take. A book that can be a harsh ride in the sense of understanding Donna's tough life situations, it has bits that will bring a smile, but it also gives detailed information on the mind and how it works. I have learnt from this book, and I have been in a very privileged position to learn directly from a great friend. Thank you, Donna!

Preface

Facing death has placed new emotional perspective on my life. It wasn't until the last trauma that I finally sat up and took back control of matters and embarked on a journey to embrace my emotions, setting out to understand who I truly was became my mission. Until then my belief was that my personality, as well as my emotional state, had become masked. We are, by default, taught to conceal our feelings in public (and often privately too) and that's not necessarily healthy. It had taken a near death experience to awaken me, force me to realise just how controlled I'd allowed myself to become and to wake the hell up.

Putting yourself first when you have four children and your eldest had a long-term boyfriend from a young age you were convinced would become your son-in-law (yup that happened) was my most difficult decision, especially so when they'd all stepped up in a time of my extreme need. However, it was time to start living in order to strive and since my head injury in April twenty-fourteen, I'd only survived in order to exist. How could that ever be good enough? Making this conscious decision felt like a weight had lifted from my shoulders and although it would mean massive changes, it would also be the beginning of my true healing process. Within me was a nagging need to become a useful mother once more and that alone was enough drive to propel me forward. This feeling was overwhelming and in order for that to happen, I first had to make sacrifices. Finally, it was time to begin liking who I'd become, despite not really being ready to do so and in accepting that the 'new' me was indeed enough (for now). I'd taken the first step in what would be an incredibly long process that I thought might only take a few months. My reality, upon reflection is that I will never be enough in my eyes.

Events that traumatise immensely deeply, the ones that remain with you throughout your lifetime and remain within your soul, continue to threaten if they are swept under the proverbial carpet, and not dealt with. Remaining an unwanted factor within your mind that continue to be a perceived threat or risk to your life they can cause a constant heightened state of hypervigilance. Causing both physical and psychological exhaustion, it isn't until you reach the point your body is in extreme pain, and you have the inability to remember important factors of your life, such as important appointments or planned events, that you realise just how much your trauma impacts on you and, just as importantly, upon your family.

Unfortunately, trauma is something that has followed me around. I've had to get to grips with it on numerous occasions throughout my life and had no choice but to crack on regardless, despite it bringing a response to a deeply distressing or disturbing event that causes an overwhelming inability to cope. Causing feelings of helplessness that diminishes a sense of self which, in turn, creates an incompetence to feel the full range of emotions and experiences, trauma has placed demands on me that ensured I'd not been capable of living a normal life. Trauma is crippling, disabling, and undignified which in turn causes feelings reaching far beyond the realms of each original incident.

Affected by underlying symptoms resulting from lived experiences, all aspects of my daily existence were showing signs of my inability to cope. Deeply troubled, my mind was in chaos as I struggled to make sense of everyday activities all of us would normally take for granted. Now I'm on top of my mental health I find it difficult to deal with anyone wishing to disrupt this balance. I have, in effect, created a zero-tolerance policy to chaos. Anyone behaving unpredictably that I consider detrimental to my well-being gets ejected, and second chances are rare. This means my life runs more smoothly and contentment is easier to attain and maintain. When trauma has touched your psyche the way it has embedded into mine, then (and only then) would I expect the understanding required to empathise with this mindset. Please understand, I'm far from intolerant; in point of fact, you'd be stretched to meet a more patient, empathetic person than me. The difference between my pre-brain trauma and post-brain trauma personality is that I'm no pushover these days. Realistically, I've grown a bigger set (psychologically speaking) than most men have and my tolerance for inappropriate (or deviant) behaviour is zilch.

I didn't survive each ordeal to remain a wimp, quivering in the shadows of my mind or indeed my home. I'm strong in body but more importantly in mind too. Folk would do well to both believe in those facts as well as remember them. Nobody gets to batter me again, either physically or emotionally. I've no intention of putting myself or my family through the tough days of PTSD a third time and I'll do all it takes to fulfil that for I know where I stand with regards to the services offered—more aptly what is and isn't available for what I might require—and that [despite law changes] nothing has physically altered at how people in my position are treated in today's modern world.

Given what will discussed in the coming chapters, let's make things clear now—at no point in my life have I considered myself a victim. My body isn't laying on a mortuary slab—I've not ended up a statistic—therefore I consider myself a survivor of the battles I've endured at the hands of others.

I'm also prepared to be a voice—an advocate—to my lived experiences, which doesn't reflect well on those that betrayed me and nor does it look good on certain authorities. There is always room for improvement and development, however and I'm prepared to step up.

Throughout this book my personal experiences of trauma are shared along with the effect these events had on me both at the time and much later in life when they manifested as Post Traumatic Stress Disorder. My diagnosis is actually Complex PTSD (which means I'm a lucky moo and have experienced long-lasting trauma with no end in sight) which, of course, comes with further complications. I'm one of the lucky ones as I've come out the other side a stronger person and I also share how and why.

Soul Searching: To PTSD Hell and Back Twice is a follow-on book to *Lost Soul: Broken Soul to Soul on Fire* in which I share my recovery journey from brain trauma. Some aspects of that journey are shared here, too, simply because my PTSD was triggered by the attack that caused it. I have attempted to address matters more deeply and from a different angle in this book to give variety rather than repetition. Living with the residing complications of brain trauma, for which medication is required, is hard graft but when the balance is right and all of it under control, there is a feeling of huge reward and self-awareness. That your own personal contribution through eating correctly, maintaining exercise and meditating has contributed alongside pharmaceuticals goes a long way in hoping that, one day, the drugs might be a long distant memory.

Through my writing, meditation, revisiting places from my past and deep-thinking techniques I am able to retrieve lost memories and because of my dedication to recovery alongside a decision made long ago to advocate my experiences, I share my story with you. I've done this in stages, as and when I feel ready. Through my insight, both as a qualified therapist and somebody suffering on the other side of matters, I hope my narrative can help others in some small way by giving them the courage to continue with their own fight.

Retrieving lost memories is a long-drawn-out process, as was learning to store new memories and being able to recall them again. Using a technique called a memory palace that replaced my conventional memory, I've gradually built up a system that works for me. Set out inside my mind much like a house, with rooms and corridors within which I place memories I'm able to store and retrieve. My system coincides with imagery around my actual home as prompts. This process will more than likely be a book in its own right one day. There are still many lost memories to recall, especially from my children's younger years and this book might reveal why that might be the case to you. Through embracing my traumas, I feel I've grown over time. Ultimately this is resultant of my lost memories returning as much as healing from the traumas themselves. I've my granddaughter to thank for much of this, for watching her bloom through each growth goal enables me to remember my own children's past. Like my own children, she exhibits strength of character and determination to strive despite her young age.

My combination of memory systems allows for an effective memory as good (sometimes better) as somebody who hasn't sustained head trauma and losses—take away my prompts and I'm left with trauma and confusion and a mind that no longer functions.

Brain trauma left me registered disabled—the attack eight years ago (on publication of this book) was brutal and most definitely left its mark on my psyche. Resulting, I'm left living with the ups and downs of complex health issues, which often give me peace or can flair simultaneously. Life, then, either continues smoothly and can is lived to the full, or it stops me in my tracks like a domino effect as serious health implications crash me to the ground as if an outside force is in control of my life.

Startingly, as a result of the number of times my life has almost ended, I'm not sure I've many (if any) chances of survival left and when I fall ill it means that I plunge into deep depression because of this. Although death doesn't worry me, I've too much living to do first.

Being a disabled person most definitely has highs and lows. Surviving was a conscious decision made during the attack in twenty-fourteen and now, as I live with the intricacies of that survival, I don't want to waste a single day. If it weren't for my family, for the grief it would have caused them the easier option, by far, would have been to have given in. As defeatist as that sounds there are still days that my pain is so intense, I cannot fathom why I'm still in existence. For this reason, I refuse to live an unfulfilled life. If I'm to endure pain either physically or when PTSD touches my life, then it must be compensated by a life worth living—one that uplifts my spirit. I've never been somebody who could sit indoors all day and do nothing, favouring to keep busy one way or another. Being housebound after my head trauma was too difficult to comprehend but I found ways to occupy my time—I truly don't think I've ever been bored my entire life and it's not something I'd ever wish to begin in my latter years—if I'm indoors, I'm writing or being artistic.

Although it feels strange to speak of my mind as extraordinary and unusual, I guess it's the best way to explain it. Unconventional is another explanation. Within the prequel to this book, my recovery was attributed to my competitiveness and to the fact that through my equine experiences I learnt to fall and stand back up. In fairness there was a triage of attributions and although I touched on my IQ it was because I thought I'd lost it. Don't get me wrong, my mathematics would let me down these days if I went for a test, but my brain works to solve issues in the same logic way as it always has. Despite my IQ being below its previous level I'm applying my learning ability (for that ability still stands) to my recovery process. This concept allows me to step up to the next level and has enabled me to strive. As you might imagine, I'm thankful this ability and inclination exists within me; my survival has depended upon my aptitude and depth of determination through my knowledge and understanding. That I know no limits has meant I can now strive. Ironically, my lived experience of traumatic events has enabled me to gain long-term psychological strength.

Go figure!

I'd like to share with you some little-known facts about Post-Traumatic Stress Disorder: that, more often than not, it affects a certain personality type. Those of us that experience it are the people who are always strong, dependable, and diligent, with a strong conscience and sense of responsibility. Yet on the inside we are the sensitive ones who are easily hurt by criticism. On the outside our self-esteem might look robust, when in reality its fragile. A person to whom you would turn in your own times of need, and who wouldn't let you down—with the attitude of 'when the going gets tough, we get going.'

Why should a person so strong be the one to get ill?

Placing stresses onto someone who is weak, or cynical, or lazy results in them immediately giving up. They will, as a result, never become stressed enough to become ill. Strong people, however, react to stress by redoubling their efforts. They push themselves beyond their limits—way beyond those designed for their body. When symptoms begin to develop, because they are sensitive and fear criticism and failure, they keep going. Something has to give way, and that's the limbic system. Inside their heads it feels like eighteen-amps pulsing through a thirteen-amp fuse, and their behaviour begins to shift.

Is it any wonder that when I am suffering there's a sharp exit from social media? A place where, in the past I have been told that, and I quote "people like you belong in those institutions, it's a shame they all closed down" or demands are made on me to buy and blog about books and then become threatening towards me if I say "no" for I'd actually like to get to the books I've read.

Overcoming adversity through trauma, without any doubt, has been my most difficult endeavour. During reflection I often question myself if survival has been worth the time, effort, and energy I now have to place into recovery. Most definitely it has, although I'm under no illusion that my journey towards recovery is far from being over. Injury aside, I'd still be striving to learn, to improve my knowledge, aspirations and seeking new experiences so why change that? Yes, I had to take a sideways step and reassess my needs but now I feel as if I'm catching up and that's a good place to be.

When it was time to place myself first, in order to recover and to become mum again, it was worth it! In doing so it felt selfish but looking back it truly wasn't as the long-term gains have been worthwhile. Once again, I can support at essential times rather than the one constantly requiring it. Although my children are now all in adulthood and have flown the nest, living independently, they couldn't be more rounded, grounded, or level-headed. Through pushing boundaries I've fought against inequality, disability, and frustration.

Soul Searching: To PTSD Hell and Back Twice is my personal story of trauma but moreover is about determination to strive over adversity—it is my story of hope and of faith. Finding the drive, energy, and confidence to recover is one matter but finding the willingness to be open regarding my whole story has been exhausting as well as uplifting. A sense of freedom has engulfed me at times—these emotions allow me to know that it's time to share.

Understanding the differences between who I was twenty years ago and now has been paramount in accepting my new identity after my assault which has helped me comprehend why my life was so devastating for so long—and why it ended in catastrophe.

Masks

Is my smile one that's fake, or one that's true,
Can you tell if I'm happy, or feeling blue?
Do my eyes sparkle from joy, or tears,
Will it be a day of laughter, or filled with fears?

Am I simply ok, or hiding behind a tough exterior,
Is my confidence genuine, or am I feeling inferior?
For every door I slam shut, am I severing connection,
Am I building a wall of protection, or avoiding rejection?

Will I stand tall, or dance behind a veil of pain,
Today might be one of freedom, or will it be a strain?
Perhaps it will be one for strength, or feeling frail,
Will it be a day in which I win, or fail?

What mask do I need today? I take a moment to wonder,
How will I cope, what pressures will I be placed under?
What will the day bring, how heavy will it weigh?
So much depends on the exterior facade I display.

Chapter One

Trauma

My personal story, regarding trauma, is long-winded for I was trapped in a cycle that seemed impossible to escape—a sequence of physical events that, thankfully, I've found a way to step beyond the grips of. That wasn't an easy task, however.

As you'll read, there were two minor incidents in my earlier years which were followed by a long-term relationship. I'm often asked why I stayed—simply put I had no idea how to leave for leaving is never simple when abuse is present in a relationship. On top of the normal concerns of where I might live and how to support myself there were also four children to consider—and there was no way I'd have left them behind.

The repeated cycle of abuse, devaluation, and positive reinforcement I was exposed to is called 'trauma bond.' Somehow, I needed to break away from this but first there was the need to struggle against the powerful emotions created when the kindness and reassurances of love kicked in. There were never any apologies (there usually are), which helped me make my decisions.

Between the 'events' happy times did prevail!

More on that in a later chapter.

Chapter Two

Childhood Views

Speaking out as a ten-year-old to a trusted member of our family, sharing with them something that hadn't sat comfortably with me that I'd believed was inappropriate (I was correct in that) resulted in me having my mouth washed out with a bar of soap. According to them, I'd 'tittle-tattled.' Children were of a generation that were seen and not heard, whereas adults swept issues under carpets. Little did I know back then that the magnitude of secrets that had been swept under the preverbal carpet had been so immense. It wouldn't be until much later into adulthood, when these secrets were shared with me, that the enormity of my insignificance that day manifested. There's no need for guilt or shame for myself, instead anger that so much had gone unsaid and un-dealt with for others. There's a time and place for other people's stories, and that's not in my book.

Instead, my part in what had occurred may have been more effective had I been listened to. Certainly, my own outlook from that point forward might have led me down a different path. Unfortunately, there were three main notions I took from my childhood—despite it being a happy, healthy, and a contented one—that nobody was prepared to listen, nobody took me seriously and that nobody believed me. Powerful concepts such as these can be catalyst for how we deal with trauma and indeed other life situations later in life.

During therapy, many years on, as intense as it was, this nougat of information wasn't disclosed because it had remained lost within the debris of my confused state that once held a memory. Notwithstanding it might have explained a great deal about me with regards to how I was now responding to the trauma I'd both experienced and my reaction to it. I am referring to the assault that disabled me. There'd be no recollection of the soap event until four years later, after visiting the place I'd witnessed the event and had a flashback memory of having my mouth washed out with soap. Moments like this stop me in my tracks, they overwhelm. After being asked if I were "okay" and having shared what was on my mind, the person I was with opened up—it was at this point I would learn the rest of the story—the magnitude of betrayal that reached far beyond anything ten-year-old me could have imagined possible. Despite how important this information is looking back upon it and understanding that recalling this during therapy would have been useful, I also realise that due to my past and the way my brain works, and given the documented evidence I hold, the wrong conclusions might well have been made. I'm thankful, then, that my recollection of some memories returned slowly, and I guess this has been for good reason—for I believe it would have complicated matters and resulted in untrue assumptions about my past. My slow retrieval (or recovery of retrograde amnesia) has been frustrating but beneficial.

Sometimes, amnesia can be useful!

Chapter Three

Amnesia

Memory loss affecting the ability to make, store and retrieve memories is called amnesia. Retrograde amnesia affects the memories formed before the onset of amnesia, whereas anterograde amnesia is to have trouble forming new memories.

Someone who develops retrograde amnesia after a traumatic brain injury (such as me) are unable to remember what happened during the years, or decades prior to that injury due to the damage caused to the memory-storage areas of the brain. This can be resultant from a traumatic injury, serious illness, seizures, stroke, or a degenerative brain disease. Progression or recovery will depend on the cause. Memory loss with retrograde amnesia involves losing facts rather than skills—so someone might forget that they own a car rather than how to drive for example.

Anterograde amnesia is when someone has trouble making new memories and accessing memories from before the onset of amnesia (which is why I made a memory palace).

These two types of amnesia can coexist in the same person, and often do.

Chapter Four

Sporty Days

Throughout my life I've been involved in many sports with my childhood filled with ponies and horses. My parents worked seriously hard for us to be able to afford this privilege, every penny went on our animals so please don't think me a spoiled brat. There were no LPs or designer clothes (or new clothes come to that unless my nanna knitted me a jumper). As I got older there was 10p a week for sweets which had to last the week (and they did). I didn't want to go to school, not because I was against learning but because the other kids wanted my money. There was no money to give, so I took the punishment. The worse bullying that I remember was one of my mum's friend's sons punching me repeatedly on the arm until a large lump appeared. His name was James.

By the time we moved house I was done with all that. A fresh start meant nobody knew what I'd been through. Somebody would only do that once and feel the force of my strength—for I did have that despite being small. After one of the lads saw for himself just how strong I was compared to him, I went back to being quiet but respected. Nobody asked to arm wrestle me for lunch money after that.

There were, of course, bumps and bruises that came part and parcel with riding horses. At fourteen I injured my back quite badly. My spine was twisted (physically) and bones in my pelvis were displaced for which there was a need for cracking and manipulation in order for realignment. This was manageable in comparison to the riding accident at sixteen that placed me in hospital and ended my competing. My horse 'Fred' and I were jumping huge courses—we were both brave and fast. On one particular day everything was going to plan until a couple of fences from the finishing line. I can only speculate that complacency or overconfidence got in my way and can share this part of my story through my witness, Mr Henry Cowell (ironically one of his sons is called Simon but not the one you are now thinking of). Henry was a well-respected gentleman from my local area in Essex who was looking after the jump where we fell—he was marking on a special card who jumped, refused, fell etc for competition officials in order for them to work out (alongside timings) who won. Each fence had someone to do this. Disaster struck when both Fred and I fell together. To this day I've no recollection of what happened beyond the approach, so my words are taken from Mr Cowell's description, and I do so with respect for not only has he passed away but at the time he thought he was dealing with a deceased body. After calling for the event ambulance using the radio Henry had been supplied, I lay motionless. Given all I was wearing it would have been highly difficult to see if I were breathing or not but there was no visible movement whatsoever.

Upon landing and falling, Fred had rolled over the top of me which would have been damaging enough, but as he stood back up the great lump used my chest as leverage. I don't remember the ambulance crew arriving, being placed on a stretcher, my mum arriving on the scene or both of us getting in the ambulance.

Unconsciousness had taken over.

At some point an image of blue lights appeared and I remember muttering "my tit hurts" before everything became black. There's nothing further until I'm in a wheelchair outside Colchester's Accident and Emergency department with my mum trying to cheer me up by doing wheelies with me waiting for dad to collect us. My God that hurt—the jarring and laughing was playing havoc with my injuries. Speaking of injuries, they were quite intense. When Fred stood on me, he pushed his studs (that I'd fitted myself) through my skin and into my flesh—horses wear studs in their shoes, much like a footballer would in their boots. Only a slight thing of a lass (about a size six at the time) and 'vertically challenged' (I am still that) my body took a battering. I'd broken both collar bones, my breast plate, and many ribs. My shoulder was also damaged. Although I healed quickly from the broken bones, there are still visible signs of the carnage if you know where to look. The lasting lung damage left me with asthma, which is aggravated by stress, damp, the cold, and smoke.

Despite wearing PPI of the horsey world, I'd gained substantial injuries. It's believed that when I woke in the ambulance and muttered those words, I was referring to my bra, the wire of which had been forced by the motion of my horse's foot from the confines of fabric into my flesh and into the hole that the studs in Fred's shoes had made.

My jockey skull cap (riding hat) had been shattered from the impact—they are designed to do that to save heads.

Bones heal but unbeknown to me this was the second score mark on my young mind. My life shifted at this point, which isn't unusual at this age, I know. Not only did I give up my passion for horses but my lifetime career goal too. Decisions were beginning to alter as life changes commenced. Unaware that fragmented nightmares that continued for many years about this accident could have been PTSD (for we'd never heard of it back then) I did what I've continued to do with my life since—

stood tall and cracked on with it. Now, with my extended knowledge of my new lived experience, I truly believe I've suffered PTSD for many years.

Again, I didn't recall this accident until after my therapy—it wasn't until I saw images of this day in my loft years later that those memories flooded back.

Chapter Five

Relationships

Already in a relationship at the delicate age of sixteen, during what is now understood to have been a raw time in my life and recovering from varying broken bones and making life-changing decisions, I was also in the partnership that would lead to marriage and take us forward into having a large family. Life continued on a path completely different to the one I'd mapped out—my riding accident changed me as a person, it changed my aspirations, and level of confidence. My assertiveness had vanished. My spirit was quenched and what I describe as my 'daredevil' self—the rider that had been born from watching Eddie Kidd (as mentioned in *Lost Soul*) faded from my psyche. The fighter attitude that once resided within me wouldn't return for many years but when it mattered, when I needed to find that fighting spirit again it was, thankfully, bursting to get out.

Meanwhile, I became impressionable. My body felt like a wreck, and with regular visits to varying medical experts to realign my spine that was still wonky, my body actually was one. Walking with a constant limp didn't do anything to help my self-esteem, neither did being continuously short of breath from my chest injuries. My past aspirations of becoming a veterinary surgeon vanished and I favoured taking secretarial subjects over scientific ones. I would be the one to remain local and not head off to university—that suited a certain person and was actively encouraged by him. Buttons were being pressed and I was too naive to know. Granted my secretarial skills have stood me well, they've been skills I've made the use of all my life.

It was a life that ticked along, behind closed doors (now there's an expression) like it tends to in situations like mine. I was in a position where he could now constantly remind me how lucky I'd been that he'd married beneath himself, living in a farmhouse, miles from civilisation.

Physical trauma didn't return to my life until several years later— 23rd January 2003 to be precise—during my pregnancy with our fourth baby. There was good reason to have left the older three children and head for the hospital in order to have both my life and that of my unborn child saved. Blood loss was substantial, after an event that caused this and the onset of early labour which commenced as a result. Labour was far too early for comfort. Both my baby and I were pumped with drugs: the priority was to give my baby steroids to develop their lungs ready for an early delivery and then to reverse labour for the sake of us both.

Doctors and midwives succeeded in doing both and over the next two months, as my baby grew inside me at an incredible rate, aided by the steroids, I can only describe that by the time she was born her strength was that of a three-month baby who looked as delicate as any new-born. Strong is an understatement—and she has continued to give me strength all her life, just as all my children have.

After the birth we were transferred to a post-natal unit, where I was reunited with the midwife that had delivered my eldest daughter seven years before. I'd refused to speak about the ordeal that had placed me in hospital two months previously but, somehow, she knew—they all knew and looking back at the damage I suffered I'm not sure why that surprised me. We spent the nights drinking tea and putting the world to rights in my curtained off cubicle at the far end of the ward. Little did I know that within this unit there were mums and babies we would know in the future. I'd never been allowed to attend anti-natal classes, so hadn't got to know anyone with all four pregnancies. When my daughter started school, these ladies knew her name and recognised me. I'd no clue who they were. As the children embarked on their education together, and I found new friends, I never shared my story of why I spent my time in hospital protecting my new baby from a cruel world instead of mixing with and getting to know them.

For that I am truly sorry.

Another name beyond my memory recall, that kind midwife has been my only therapy for this trauma despite having asked for it. My need for tea during such unsociable hours has stemmed from these days too, knowing this was the only way to soothe my mind from the ordeal—it isn't lost on me, upon reflection, that during my most recent PTSD when my nightmares were about this subject, that tea was what soothed me during my crisis months.

'Behind closed doors' is an expression worth returning to, for it's not talked about enough. From the other side of my closed doors, it would have appeared as if normal family life existed, when in reality I lived a completely separated and isolated life. My parents weren't welcome although they still came. I was forbidden to see my cousin, Emma for ten long years. My duty was the children and the house, and of course to have the dinner on the table at set times. He had nothing to do with any of the aforementioned, for they were 'chores' beneath his standing.

My escape was running, and nobody seemed under any illusion that due to the weight loss that went alongside it, something was amiss.

When, finally, I was back in touch with my cousin things were beginning to change for me—I was finding an inner strength I'd forgotten existed.

In April two-thousand-and-six I finally found the strength to walk away and did that with one suitcase between myself and my four children. We had the dog in tow too.

I feel I've been fighting since. Sometimes physically.

Of course, the stories flew around. That's called transference. Words that did nothing to prepare me for what I was about to face.

Without much to rent in the area, I'd taken a key to a barn conversion, and we squatted until something became available. Making it an adventure for the children, it was the first move of five in less than a year in an attempt to stay a step ahead.

Chapter Six

Trauma Bonding

Two people that undergo intense, risky emotional experiences can develop trauma bonding. In the context of abusive relationships this bond becomes stronger due to heightened intimacy and danger. Similar to the way Stockholm Syndrome manifests—when hostages form a bond with their captors—the abused forms bonds with the abuser as both sources of terror, but more importantly for them, the comfort that enables them to survive is supplied by them too. Resulting is an unshakeable sense of loyalty and devotion to the abuser that appears obviously irrational from the outside.

Often the abuse comes in cycles of extreme violence followed by the rescue phase—this is a particularly fierce and repetitive situation of seduction and betrayal. Those that abuse in this way convey elements of kindness, nobility and righteousness who wish to stay involved with those they abuse and who, after the event when their 'victim' leaves, believe they are the ones who've betrayed them. They share exploitation, fear, and danger wishing to inflict emotional pain, severe consequences and even the prospect of death.

Intermittent reinforcement—in the context of psychological abuse—is vindictive and insensitive treatment that is also mixed with random bursts of affection. Physical rewards are gifted unpredictably throughout the abuse cycle—a dinner out or flowers for example—leaving the abused perpetually seeking approval whilst settling for the occasional display of positive behaviour towards them (for there was a honeymoon phase in their relationship that drew them in initially).

Manipulation is key to the games an abuser plays, in whatever situation they are in (husband/wife, parent/child are two examples). Every small but rare positive behaviour is achieved in an amplified manner, often described as the 'small kindness perception.' In threatening and survival situations, evidence of hope is a small sign that a situation might improve—and this is what we hang onto.

Biochemistry plays an important role in narcissistic abuse (for this is what is truly going on). I go into detail on why chemicals affect our brain and body in more detail later in the book which will give you more clarity on this, but in the meantime, biochemical addiction is involved when it comes to intermittent reinforcement and trauma bonding—and when oxytocin, serotonin, dopamine, cortisol, and adrenaline are involved with abuse natured relationships it can result in strengthening them, rather than dampening them. The bond is therefore due to a chemical reaction rather than wanting to endure the behaviour. It creates an addiction not unlike a drug addiction—imagine how difficult it is, then, to break free of an abusive relationship.

Chapter Seven

Looking Over My Shoulder

Moving from address to address is hardly the stability a mother wants for her children. As soon as it was possible, I purchased what would become our long-standing, permanent home. We filled the walls with our own artwork and photography, we gathered around the dining room table each evening to deliberate how each of our days had gone. Over time I taught my children the wonderful art of debate, to stand for their beliefs and to argue their point but also to take on board and consider counterarguments. They were also taught to get out there and fight for their education. Each have gone on and sought degrees. Some have gone on to reach for a master's degree too. Mostly we filled our hearts with love.

Our home became our castle, it was our sanctuary—and that's what we required above all else for my stalker was placing all of us under immense pressure. He'd been on my case three weeks after I left my ex, and it was relentless. Most women know their stalkers—a phenomenon usually personal and they are the most dangerous kind.

I'm thankful for my children's repressed memories and my resilience, for it means, despite all I went through, they were still able to have a relationship with their father rather than my other option of being removed by Women's Aid and taking on another life.

Quickly learning that there was a need to stand on my own two feet, for the authorities believed that there was a basic human right for this person to be outside my home, there was no choice other than for me to 'grow a set.' I knew this was wrong on every level and because I'd undertaken a criminology degree, knew Paladin was on its way and also knew Laura Richards' name. Alone I stood, collecting my own evidence in order that, eventually the stalking and harassment would stop.

Stop it did.

After six long years.

Losing count how many times the locks were changed as well as both my mobile phone numbers and land line, sometimes weekly, I begun to lose trust in who conversations could be held with, or who I allowed access to my home. Being stalked caused paranoia and to a degree has created certain routines that still exist within my life. A stickler for not sticking to routine with regards to times to leave or return home and for having the curtains closed as soon as darkness falls became two rules of the house. Another that phones were not allowed at the table during meals and to be honest that's just good old-fashioned manners.

For us, each phone in the house would ring in turn every time we sat down at the table each morning and evening to eat, until one was answered. If it wasn't answered, the calls were relentless, from one phone to the next, to the next, to the next and on it went. We varied the times, yet that didn't deter. The silent mode was applied to all phones, and I insisted we talked and ate behind drawn curtains. It became my children's time to shine in conversation—and boy can they talk!

After six years of being stalked, I was in a position of being able to learn the process of relaxation. That's not something I'm great at still in all honesty for it followed a harrowing total of nine years of constant battles of survival—of trauma—with my only rest-bite being my work as a photographer in Kent and London. I have worked hard at putting these experiences behind me. I've forgiven everyone involved (for there are multiple people I'm talking about that got sucked into certain events) and drawn a line under this period in my life. As far as I'm concerned, physically, this is water under the bridge.

When new events in your life echo old ones and the actions of others begin to repeat behaviours that you've previously been exposed to (despite them being directed towards a third party) anxiety becomes difficult to control. When anxious thoughts begin to come true within your new life (and there's only a 1% chance of that occurring) more often than the anxiety being just unnecessary 'worry' then there's a huge problem going on. Unsurprisingly this triggered my PTSD and in November twenty-twenty my life spiralled out of control.

During this latest episode of PTSD, I attempted to seek therapy and I share the outcome of that in the chapter 'My Relationship With Therapy' in order that subjects remain grouped together.

It wasn't pretty.

Chapter Eight

At The Scene

Continuing with my experiences with trauma, there have been several horrific scenes witnessed over the years, simply because I happened to be there as they unfolded. I've attended major road traffic accidents at which there's been a need for me to administer emergency first aid. In my younger years I was qualified to do this—certainly not to the level of a paramedic but I've saved lives non-the-less. Not everyone lived long enough to require help for long and these are the scenes that stick in your mind the most as, while you are helping, a life slips away.

Within *Lost Soul* I share a story about a cyclist who gets hit by a car while I'm waiting for a bus. While I hold his skull together, with blood and brain matter covering my hands, a large chunk of my memory returns. I've no indication if this man—Derek—lived or not and often find myself thinking about him and the outcome of his life (or death). Closure is important and despite it being none of my business, I don't have it. This bothers me no end, keeping me awake at times.

Some of the other sights I've seen have been used in my novels already. The accident (less the gunshot wounds) that kills 'Charlie' in *Broken* during a car chase in Scotland was based on a young driver that rolled his car (nose to tail) a couple of times while I was taking my children to their Essex schools one morning. First on the scene I was expecting a tree branch to have gone through this lad's head for it had penetrated the car windscreen at the correct point. Thankfully, it only grazed the top of it. He'd broken glass in his eyes and was high on whatever he'd taken—the adrenaline wasn't helping him either. A lucky escape for him and I hope he's turned his young life around.

Another will be featured in a future book. A gory sight I witnessed on the A13 one Boxing Day that I'll not share for now as I'm keeping it real in the book.

These gory sights stick in your mind—they affect your psyche more than you realise despite them not being personal to you. Often, they remain in the background until an event affects you or someone close to you does something that brings them to the surface. It wasn't until twenty-twenty that these road traffic accidents appeared in my nightmares, after my partner was involved in a crash with a lorry (I wasn't in the car with him). With my PTSD already triggered they were now affecting me on a deep and personal level.

Morality can hit hard when you least expect it too!

It is worth noting here that trauma doesn't have to be a personal experience for it to trigger PTSD and nor does PTSD have to follow a textbook, beginning three months after an event. The first RTA I witnessed was right back in two-thousand-and-nine and it had taken eleven years before it manifested as PTSD. On the flipside, I was a passenger in an accident at a very young age, this has never affected me, appeared in dreams, or caused flashbacks. Go figure!

Chapter Nine

Illness

Twenty-ten was the last time I was ill with fever (until very recently, when as a side effect of my anti-seizure medication, I was diagnosed with kidney stones that I'd started passing). I'd had a run of tonsillitis but this time there was an allergic reaction to penicillin and the throat infection caused an abscess called Quinsy. This is a rare and potentially serious complication of tonsillitis. I was also suffering from the allergic reaction, so my throat was closing due to that—the abscess burst causing a huge risk of sepsis. All this was a little close to the brain for comfort and I was rushed to hospital. As soon as the infection subsided, they whipped my tonsils out and I can honestly say I've fought external infection since—I've had one cold for one day post that date despite my immune system being compromised from the medications I now take.

I'd used another a life token. I'm not sure how many I've been issued!

Twenty-thirteen saw me taking on a job that meant taking risks every time I turned up for a shift, fulfilling my adrenaline requirements perfectly (there's a chapter dedicated to that). It was here that I was bitten by another human being within three weeks of my employment commencing—this had been the last time I was given antibiotics under strict restrictions, again until recently. My reactions were not at all good but the blood clot that had formed at the wound site was causing concern.

Reflection is a wonderful hindsight, and I wished now, that I'd walked away from the employment then.

Until the kidney stones, this bite was the worse pain I'd ever experienced. In comparison—as explained to the A&E surgeon—the pain from the bite went eventually but from the stones, it was relentless (pain that lasted months). For a long time, the pain from the bite sat at 8/10 compared to the stones at ten, but that has shifted since.

I didn't leave. Instead, I endured. Seeing this forensic mental health behavioural unit as a challenge, an environment in which I was thriving professionally, it is fair to say as much as this job gave me satisfaction it was becoming apparent the risks were far outweighing what the job was worth to me. Not so long after this first incident, I was on the receiving end of a bleach attack, my eyesight was risked but knowing how to deal with that was a massive bonus. Drenching my eyes in running, tepid water for half an hour before heading to the hospital saved my sight. The person (who was out of prison on licence) returned to prison for this attack. She had only been where I worked as no other place could handle her. There was a court case and in her statement to the police she had said she'd wished she'd had shot me in the eye. When asked in court what the consequences would have been had they have shot me in the head, they were aware that would have killed me. While the trial date was upcoming, my boss wouldn't allow this person to be moved or held in police custody as the company would have lost money—I had to work in the same building and often in the same room as this person, a person who had also accused a colleague of sexual abuse (proven to be false). My physical safety was compromised for several months. This highly stressful time had an impact, and once they had been sentenced, overtime lacked which suddenly became my fault. Being under pressure from a lot of angles took a toll, it felt like I was being punished for following protocol in a tough environment—one in which the environment catered for those too damaged to allow into society or were lacking capacity to stand trial (they would have been a danger to both themselves and to the public if released). Upon her release from prison to a less secure setting, there was a twenty-five-mile exclusion zone put in place that they breached, and I came face-to-face with them locally. Needless to say, this was a surreal day. They were still on licence and the authorities were fast to act in removing the person to a new location—I do know where because of my contacts through other means (although I shouldn't) and she won't be released anytime soon. These two smaller traumas haven't caused me too much issue, psychologically, although I do sometimes get nightmares with regards to an acid attack from a faceless person and I believe it obvious where this 'dream' stems.

Ironically, I'd already started putting out the feelers to change this job, but that change hadn't occurred before being attacked a third time. This is the incident I talk about openly online and through my recovery story within my book, *Lost Soul*. The injuries I sustained in twenty-fourteen during my last trauma have been life-changing. Brain trauma has left me fighting several battles both internally on a psychological level and also physically. Not least this relentless attack, during which I was punched six times in the head (and the back of it slammed against a wall) leaving me feeling as if I'd entered a boxing ring without any training and no way of being able to defend myself—legally I couldn't retaliate. The irony is certainly not lost on me that the man who so severely attacked me was allowed, on occasion, into the community (all be that accompanied). One particular time I was in a shop with my youngest daughter when I heard his voice. Without hesitation I sent her away, not wanting her seen with me, but he'd clocked us. Every time he saw me in the work environment thereafter all he focused on was my daughter's "beautiful legs"—he was a man obsessed. She'd just turned eleven years old. Within weeks this notion had frustrated the man to boiling point, despite me remaining professional and as I'd always done, not disclosed any personal information or let any of them in either emotionally or personally in any way—and that included him. Despite being asked from day one if I'd a family, I'd refused to answer, and this continued still. A colleague had even showed this man where I lived—my old boss, upon my complaint, had verbally snapped at me that he may as well have led him to my daughter's bedroom door (although given the circumstances that unfolded, I'd expect she'd deny those words now).

Unfortunately, I wasn't wearing a personal mobile alarm (I've not disclosed this in writing until now, but it was mentioned in my interview with Frank Portinari at the end of December twenty-twenty-one) as none of them worked. The fixed wall alarms were faulty too, sending colleagues to the incorrect room in emergencies. I have documentation proving this from the local council as such places are funded by taxpayers and thus safety features affecting everyone involved is very much their business. By the time help arrived it was too late, and I'd taken charge of the situation. Long story short, if I'd have fallen to the floor, I would have died but that day wasn't my time—it was, however too late for me. Although it would be a few days before the impact of that day would catch up with me, my injuries were substantial and the magnitude of consequences of a sick individual who had targeted my eleven-year-old and taken out his frustrations on me would change my life forever.

Taking days to process the damage, my brain eventually shut down in a major way. The three weeks recovery from concussion that I'd been diagnosed was far from my reality. Internally it felt as if doors were closing on my mind—and as each one shut my life became further out of reach. My memory faded until there was nothing to see, feel or think except to experience the physical pain and to endure it. A lifetime of nothing. No past, present or future. Isolation. A prison inside my head. A feeling of ever decreasing circles as I was dragged beneath the surface and suffocated by my existence.

When I woke up—I was nothing and knew nobody.

Now registered disabled, I'm still working to regain parts of me that are buried deep and will never give up until each section of my brain has healed. I've come such a long way already, but the darker days let me know there's still a long winding voyage ahead of me before my healing journey is finally over—I'm optimistic by nature yet I truly believe it's a road I'll be travelling until the end and I'm okay with that.

One of my disabilities caused by head trauma is being left to cope with seizures. The cocktail of medications I take to control these, along with a healthy diet and exercise all contribute to keeping them under control. There's also the need to stay away from certain situations such as constant television, flashing lights, sunlight through trees whilst moving past, lines/patterns that appear to move and infection (such as kidney infections that accompany my kidney stones). I also need ample sleep. There are a couple of things I've had to give up due to seizures too, one is alcohol which I can live with, and the other is driving. I get to the latter later.

Through having a healthy lifestyle, it has been possible to eradicate seizures from an average of seven (major ones) weekly to having them controlled—until things go wrong and when they do begin to go wrong, I struggle to accept these changes in the same way I struggled to accept the way my life had been stolen from me after the assault. My whole personality, purpose and capability changed due to being assaulted and to have my seizures out of control is the beginning of my life becoming a huge mess—of my memory beginning to fail and a downwards tumble towards depression.

Depression weakens my reserve, and this is when I'm most vulnerable to having flashbacks. In my case they are often triggered by an event that might not be related to the original trauma. For me, returning to hell the first time was triggered by someone in a swimming pool, innocently taking his child swimming and larking around. Because of an innocent act on this person's part, my flashbacks commenced—and yes it would have been triggered at some point, I'm sure of that. I'd personally have preferred that to have been someplace else, as everyone believes my first tonic clonic seizure also occurred in that pool at that moment. I was pulled from beneath the water by a lifeguard and remember the burning sensation as I coughed up pool water. After this incident, my fear of water exhibited, and it took a long time (and therapy) to resolve this.

As a result of my head injury trauma, I have been all the way to hell and back to resolve PTSD—it was far from an easy journey—and now, as the title of this book indicates, I have been to hell and back a second time—and in all honesty it is somewhat difficult and unfathomable to comprehend that this time it was caused by someone I've not even met.

Occasionally in life there's someone determined to destroy what you've created. As an individual it fractures your very being as you feel yourself descend into the depths of hopelessness. There's a huge positive come from this second experience however, and if I've learnt anything from my second encounter with the devastating symptoms of PTSD then that's of the strength between my partner, myself, and our relationship—not only for the love and friendship we have as a couple but the bond we've created as we've risen above all we've endured. Thus, we know that to have been through so much so early on and to have survived what was planned to destroy us, we can move forward in the knowledge we are forever. That's a wholesome feeling, to know love without boundaries—love that's unconditional.

Before this realisation, calm was far from my agenda and flashbacks of my past begun. Never had I thought it possible that I'd be giving someone from my previous life power over my mind years after peace had fallen between us, yet it was happening. Strange feelings were taking over my existence causing me distress, discomfort, and constant hypervigilance. Since my head injury I've struggled with claustrophobia, and this was clouding my emotions. I'm unsure what was more suffocating, enclosed spaces or the shame that mounted up but with each week that passed and the deeper my suffering, the further my feelings were buried until it got to the point that numbness took over. When you no longer feel joy in the things that normally you'd love participating in, what's the point anymore? I was setting about each day existing somewhere in my life and regardless of the fact I was physically there, my soul had once more been misplaced. Despair followed me like an unwanted shadow, my only reaction was to burst into tears and to not be able to explain why.

At least I recognised the signs. Chaos had returned to my life, and I was once again in need of seeking clarity.

Everyone assumed my flashbacks were relating to the head injury and as an expert in avoidance, I didn't feel any need to correct them. The real reason wasn't something that was going to be a family discussion and I certainly cannot start talking about them in detail on social media. With nowhere to turn, I found myself living within a world of silence. Of course, there was always the option to share the burden with my other half, for he was sharing his with me. Imagine if you would, the dilemma I faced each night, waking from extreme nightmares, only to face flashbacks of someone that had caused me such harm so many years ago and for such a lengthy duration—a period in which I'd often wondered if I'd survive, while the man I love slept beside me. How could I bring something like that into a relationship? Even worse into the bed we share!

We were already going through a different kind of hell.

I've already explained that the professional help I'd booked into rejected me. I'd never felt so abandoned—which is a common emotion of PTSD and one that I experience regularly.

Ironically, some of the routines that affect me as a result of being stalked are also major aspects for those who suffer with PTSD. The feeling of being watched, for example, is a strong symptom of the disorder and although this isn't a factor for me whilst feeling well it most certainly is during times of crisis while my symptoms are flaring and the dark cloud that seems to arrive begins to swamp my mind—some around me don't seem to understand why I suffer depression or why I am fine one day and wake with it the next. In describing what it feels like from within, I feel like there's a crack in the earth so deep and dark ready to swallow me up unannounced. The sensation of falling through this crack is that of drowning and the light being drawn from my soul to be replaced with a heaviness that drags me down further. Depression doesn't really describe how it makes me feel personally, although, I guess it's as close as I will get to a diagnosis—and I have been diagnosed with depression (which is also a side effect of two of the medications I take and also two anaemias I have). This feeling runs much deeper than that. My 'depression' feels different to how other people without PTSD describe it, firstly it lasts much longer but, and I believe it's due to the many years of trauma I've sustained (please bear in mind I've not described nine years' worth of it) I have a diagnosis of Complex Post-Traumatic Stress Disorder. Although there are many symptoms added to PTSD in diagnosing CPTSD these are the ones that affect me personally: for starters I have difficulty controlling my emotions and that applies to my whole life, symptomatic with PTSD or not; I'm naturally drawn towards distrusting new people or world situations; feelings of hopelessness engulf me with ease despite my attempts to stop this from happening and this in turn causes me to believe that I'm permanently damaged; there's also an overwhelming notion that I'm completely different from other people to the point they don't understand me, my feelings, or my experiences (unless they've been through similar trauma); this all makes for difficult intimate relationships; and when PTSD flairs, as do my pain levels.

Incidentally, in line with my feeling of awake sensations of drowning my dreams at night are of falling into water (falling dreams often occur as anxiety dreams in many of us but we don't hit the floor). Unfortunately—and I've been informed its rare—I both hit the surface of the water and disappear underneath it.

Traumatic experiences cannot be changed, they form part of who you are and become embedded as part of you. History cannot be re-written, and so it is important to embrace your past rather than deny it happened—that would be denying yourself a future. Acceptance is the first step to recovery, however difficult a process that might be. Contrastingly, I've been told on many occasions that if I let go of my past and move on, my life would be easier, but reality isn't that simple. In advocating my past, it helps me live a fulfilling future. Trauma physically grips tightly onto your psyche and that's where the issue lays—bottling it up is not the healthy alternative. You have to put in a huge effort to gain a balance. Talking enables but you do need to select the correct audience. Not everyone is equipped to listen, understand, or indeed cope with what you have to say. Knowing when to stop is as equally important as knowing when to talk. As a guide, a therapist would listen for an hour per week (and receives supervision). If you find yourself needing to vent about issues for prolonged periods, lasting hours, to ease the burden of your own mind, then it is time to seek professional help.

Posting on social media about my lived experiences has helped many people and that's wonderful. I'm well practiced in what to say, and more often than not I share a passage from my published works. Sometimes not, and instead share spontaneous messages of hope. In either case my words are written gently and well received and not intended to make others feel overwhelmed or uncomfortable in any manner. My point is that while writing about trauma or speaking of it in any circumstance you cannot do so in a way that causes someone else trauma as a result and you must be mindful of this.

One way in which I've dealt with my injury and recovery was to write *Lost Soul*, which also benefitted others. There must, then, be a time and place and it should always be appropriate and not distressing. Conversations cannot impact on others in a way that manifest consequences and thus you cannot offload your troubles onto someone who isn't equipped to deal with them—you cannot rant without also giving closure and a way out. Here rests one of my many issues, and I did address this in the first book to a degree. I am trained to deal with the troubles of others as I'm a qualified psychotherapist. For some reason I can be sat anywhere in public, and strangers pour their hearts out to me. As far as I'm aware, "Free Therapy" has never been tattooed across my forehead, yet folk seem to queue up to transfer their issues onto me. That's just dandy when I'm going through the mill myself and have nowhere to take my own issues—I no longer have the support of supervision (chit chat for the therapist) so the buck stops with me. When my lake is overfilling and the dam is about to burst it is always me left not sleeping, worrying about everyone else's problems with nobody to talk to about my own. On many occasions I've been told to dismiss my anxiety or when I've attempted to talk about it, the conversation is immediately twisted into theirs, or worse still a blame game. For the record I own my anxiety when it happens and seriously cannot help it. During moments of extreme stress, however I struggle to string sentences together and that's due to the chemical releases going on in my body interfering with my ability to function correctly. At this point I've been pushed too far psychologically, and conversation needs to wait.

Feelings of isolation when you're at a low ebb is a lonely place, but somehow, I manage to get through. Sometimes I don't know how.

After the assault in twenty-fourteen my life became a series of "I can't do that anymore's" for it changed who I was and also my ability. It took years to change my perspective on life and now it's a matter of "I'll try this instead." Near death experiences do change you and I wish I'd had the help to show me that my life was a series of "firsts" rather than lasts. Focussing on and putting effort into setting goals, and attaining them, has become important to me and is most definitely what works for me in pushing myself beyond boundaries to heal these days.

From Chaos

Blinded by your rage, a storm within your mind,
Lost within a fog, clarity difficult to find.
Your mind a whirlpool, the darkness like a disease,
Chaos crushing your soul, bringing you to your knees.

The feeling you're drowning, fills your heart with sorrow,
Praying day by day, that it gets better tomorrow.
That the water so deep, muddy, and murky,
Slowly begins to clear because you know you're worthy.

That the burdens carried, weighing you down heavily,
Gradually get lifted, something you need dreadfully.
As clarity follows chaos, and order is restored,
Breathe deeply, you've a new journey to be explored.

Chapter Ten

Self-Reflection

Self-reflection is a vital aspect of my daily life. It doesn't matter how busy I become, or how many demands are placed upon me, this essential time is placed aside in order for me to preserve my well-being. Not everyone in my life understands the ramifications of interrupting this time, or how complex it has become, as I slip into deep meditation afterwards. I'm often jerked back into reality without the gentle steps back that are recommended. For me this makes my heart rate escalate and puts my brain in instant hyper-vigilant mode. That's not a good basis for discussing what might be on their agenda. Interruptions such as this are actually dangerous for me for two reasons. Firstly, if I've fallen asleep (yes, I do that) the sudden awakening from such a deep place can cause me to disassociate (have an outer body experience); or secondly, a seizure. There's mixed evidence on meditation and epilepsy and more research is required in order to establish a link between the two but I know the more I meditate the more seizures I get. I also know that without meditation my memory issues don't get resolved.

Through writing I've discovered a no-fear approach to emotion and thus a relief to my darkest or most pain-struck days. It is on the toughest days that I've authored my favourite poems or most poignant scenes within my novels. These are the times I'm at my deepest and most meaningful when it comes to thought through writing, for I don't fear vulnerability. Instead, I'm learning to tap into my inner self in order to vanish whatever holds me back vocally. This is a powerful notion that's been accomplished through the power of the keyboard despite the tough times when the negative emotions such as despair encompass me. Through my keyboard I am, then, relearning who I am and discovering what my life is about. Writing enables me to fulfil my purpose and, through beginning to understand who I am, permits me to fit into society again. This is how I've learnt to live my best life—and help others do the same.

I'd lost all that through brain trauma.

Quite astonishing, when you think about it—I wanted to become a veterinary surgeon yet 'psychologically battered' into secretarial work. It's true what they say, the [metaphorical] pen is mightier than the sword.

Not every day can or will be okay, and once that's accepted life does begin to take a turn for the better and you can commence to embrace the uphill struggle of conquering fears and phobias. Fear engulfed me far too many years through reaction but also the ramification of my children knowing my truth—and I hid that from them over nineteen years before speaking out. Frankly, I believed them knowing the truth would produce more questions than it answered and in some instances it did. In time, it will produce more.

Embracing emotions, I'm sure you've worked out, through the written word, it appears, is far simpler for me. Sitting down and discussing them is awkward and challenging for it forces me to come to terms with parts of me I've yet to rediscover. Through writing I'm able to establish a relationship with myself again, to regain a sense of self once more and get to know myself at a deep level—and from the response I get on-line when I share my work and words where they've touched others as well as taught them what it's like living with various illnesses, giving a deep understanding of how, perhaps a loved one, might feel—which is humbling.

Twenty-nineteen was the year that I made a conscious decision to become an advocate for speaking out about the mental health complexities head trauma left me facing. Talking about PTSD, seizures and memory loss became a regular feature on Instagram and Facebook and still are to this day. One post I shared gained the attention of Headway, The Brain Injury Association which resulted in my story being shared on their website. This, in turn gained national attention from the press and within weeks my story was shared nationally in the METRO. Twenty-twenty-two now becomes the year I speak out about rape, domestic abuse, and stalking (and how easy it is to be trapped within a negative cycle). Becoming an advocate has been tremendously rewarding. Not only have there been therapeutic benefits for myself, but I've received many messages of thanks and encouragement. Turning negative experiences into positive ones in this way gives me hope that I can make someone else's life a little more comfortable. This far outweighs the few that would rather I stop sharing my life so willingly for that's not going to happen for several reasons. Notwithstanding, the fact that my life was once super controlled and won't be again. Not only does this deep reflection help me build a better future, as I've mentioned, but it also helps me to manage the physical pain I now suffer and have to live with as it puts me in a psychologically strong position—in turn this releases the correct chemicals that help reduce my pain levels. Furthermore, I get to help others, which is priceless.

Emotion is and always will be something that takes all of us by surprise. After all there are many different ones for us to get to grips with. Taking the rough with the smooth is something we all have to cope with and when fear entered my life again it did so with gusto. Here's a list of a few emotions: admiration, adoration, aesthetic appreciation, amusement, anxiety, awe, awkwardness, boredom, calmness, confusion, craving, disgust, empathetic pain, entrancement, envy, excitement, fear, horror, interest, joy, nostalgia, romance, sadness, satisfaction, sexual desire, sympathy, and triumph—that's a lot to be dealing with.

Most of my physical issues stem from damaged nerves, for which time has been a great healer. There are periods in my life when my old strength and self actually begin to re-emerge. Relapses occur from time to time, it's part of the territory (even though I might not like it) that vary in severity—these times add to the risk of my mental health being under threat, which is my responsibility to correct and to ensure I look after myself when the heaviness of the dark cloud begins to press heavily on my shoulders. I'm not willing to allow the shadow that pulls me towards the crack in the ground and into the abyss to control my life to the point that PTSD is around the corner, and when I'm in excruciating pain or depressed I know that to be the case.

Life can be extremely hard.

During times of distress, I am likely to isolate myself from social media. I'd never felt the need to retract for nine months before, but the last time was different and occurred for two reasons. Foremost there was a need to lock down Facebook (now Meta) in order that old photo albums are no longer accessible other than to my children and myself. This isn't reflective on the friends I have, please allow me to make that very clear. For a long time now, my children and I haven't interacted on my timelines and there's purpose for this—since my head injury and becoming an author they got a hard time being approached by various strangers. They were young and none of us were going to tolerate it. We've stuck to this principle. Secondly, as a specialist in human behaviour I'd noted that every time I posted something positive it was having detrimental bearing on another situation my partner and I were facing. All the effort it had taken building up my social media presence was halted in hope this would stop—my book sales plummeted and of course we were in lockdown, so I wasn't able to attend book events and public speaking functions that I'd become accustomed to. I started to concentrate, instead, on healing from PTSD and working behind the scenes on website design. Of course, I was working on this book too. Furthermore, Dave and I began a secret project together that took up time during lockdown, that we'll be excited to share once it's completed. It became my habit not to look online and slowly, I am returning.

Writing continues to dominate my spare time. Not only does it open up opportunities, but it enables me to remember my life and to heal. There has been so much help for me to recall and store the negative content of my past, that in order for me to be able to move forward there was a need to create positive memories too. For too many years all I could recall was violence, which was difficult to comprehend. Living with such negativity during twenty-seventeen almost swallowed me so on New Year's Eve I decided that Twenty-Eighteen was the year in which to make positive memories. My social media posts were about family gatherings and special events. These were among the posts I've locked, but they showed me how my life was about setting goals I wasn't sure were attainable and how the possibility I'd fail far outweighed the chance of achievement. I am a risk-taker and every risk I took paid off, thankfully.

Travelling alone was the largest risk considering my health and it still is. I'd decided that life was for living: what was the point in having survived if only to exist? Travelling alone is not recommended for someone like me due to my inability to multi-task and the risk of having seizures. Anxiety does become a factor for the daunting and dangerous prospect of such situations because so much can go so drastically wrong. In overcoming that, I've learnt to place my faith in the transport system and those working for them, for at times I've not had a choice but to travel alone. Over time I have learnt that communication is key to survival and that to meet my needs on such days is to speak out as transport staff are trained to deal with folk like me. That said, the company of someone you trust is far more pleasant than feeling panicked over missing your station.

When these new memories were being made, I still required more. My family still needed more from me (not that they ever asked for it). Yet without access to the photographs of memories from our past, some of my goals have been impossible to achieve. The small snippets I'd restored of my children's younger years have been from our conversations and limited photographs that my parents have. Often conversations alone are not enough: imagine throwing sloppy paint and having it hit a blank canvas and it is sliding off. I can see the pain and disappointment in their eyes when they know something isn't resonating.

Although heart breaking and soul destroying, I cannot let it destroy me. I've never been allowed copies of the photographs that I took as the children grew up during their younger years, and for me being denied these 'memories' means there is no way I can work on retrieving them for myself now. Sometimes in life, you just have to let go.

Memories

Close your eyes and you will see
Snippets of the past, of you and me.
Relax your body, soul, and mind
Deep within your being, memories you'll find.

I no longer weep for what I can't recall
Those times from when you were so small.
Time to let go, to move on
New beginnings, a new song.

Yet so often, I'll surprise you
With something obscure, a memory not new.
Something from our past
A snippet of me and you.

Chapter Eleven

My Relationship with Therapy

An avid believer in therapy I placed my trust in a young lady in the beginning after my head trauma. She had me reliving my attack week after week, going over every minute detail. Trauma has a beginning, middle and an ending so the events leading up to the attack, the attack itself and the aftermath needed to be discovered as all I could recall was a tiny segment. We repeated this process until I could deal with it in an unemotional manner—not crying my way through. She taught me to detach myself from my emotions with regards to that day.

I didn't need help detaching from emotion so found that the easiest task in the world imaginable. Up went an imaginary brick wall—that included towards her as she also wanted to quench my competitiveness towards healing—nobody gets to crush my spirit again and as that was one of the only parts of my identity remaining, I rejected her.

Needless to say, my PTSD continued and a few months down the line there was need of further intervention. Enter Gary who transformed my life. He wanted to do a little time travelling and each week I returned we went a little deeper into my life as well as concentrating on the here and now. That was two types of therapy in one session each week. Hard work pays off if you're prepared to put in the work. Still, there wasn't time to cover it all as there were some pressing issues holding me back in my daily life that needed addressing. His threat that he'd come swimming with me was enough to drive me into the water on one of the coldest days in an unheated pool—and to read that story you'll need to do so in *Lost Soul*. Gary called that self-harm at our next session (I called it determination), but I also called it dignity for he was the type of person who didn't give empty threats—I recognise folk like that as I'm one of them! Gary and I didn't return to ten-year-old me and the bar of soap—a notion I've often wondered what conclusions he'd have come to. I vowed to share it if I ever bumped into him—which is unlikely now I've moved.

As promised earlier in the book, I will share my latest encounter with therapy and that isn't a positive experience. Extreme nightmares and flashbacks were manifesting during the night in an unpredictable manner—I'd not know what to expect as there were so many different events over the course of nine years. Not knowing when or being able to see an end in sight to prolonged trauma is the reason I'm diagnosed with Complex Post-Traumatic Stress Disorder. Not being able to predict which incident my night would take me to within a distressing nine-year period was devastating—at least first time around I knew it would be the assault without flexibility. This was different. Erratic.

The therapist had made up her mind that I needed to concentrate on reliving rape in order that I could stop the fragmented flashbacks of it. My reality was that that part was occurring in nightmares and certainly wasn't fragmented: I could and do remember every sordid detail and consequence. I had told her who, when, how, and why I thought it had happened—the smells I remembered and the reasons why hospitalisation wasn't immediate despite blood loss during pregnancy and the early onset of labour. What was required was to master the anxiety, which in turn would balance the chemicals inside my brain (and I get to the science later in the book). There was also an urgent need to focus on the flashbacks and come to terms with some of the other events that had happened during the stalking years—focussing on rape, I believe would have ticked a box and given career progression whereas there is nobody qualified to deal with stalking.

I was therefore dismissed, despite being diagnosed with clinical depression, clinical anxiety, and Complex PTSD.

Hung out to dry, alone and in despair my only option was to help myself. Imagine being in this position and not know anything about your condition. For me, at least there was another avenue to turn to and faced with these circumstances, I turned to books. These were in plentiful supply on my shelves and my kindle but deciding there was a need for a fresh perspective I undertook some research. This isn't something I'd recommend to anyone if I'm honest—self-therapy—but I am also a qualified psychotherapist. I purchased a new collection of books from several professionals and my quest begun.

There was also additional research for medication, which I did and ran past my doctor. It met with approval but it's not a solution I'm willing to share as it was very much 'outside the box' thinking and a personal risk I was willing to take. Although this solution has worked at keeping my adrenaline in check and there isn't a risk of addiction, there is of course a risk of dependency. Having been on the medication for over a year and knowing that coming off them might cause drastic effects (and having been told not to) I do have to wonder just how long I might have to remain reliant upon them.

In the meantime, the combination of these new tablets and the books I was now reading and working through, meant there was slow progress on recovery. The numbness subsided slowly and as I functioned in a more normal and accepting manner—I could start to feel the progress within myself. The times I found myself bursting into my daughter's room in the early hours because in my head she was screaming because she'd been raped, lessened. The quantity of times of being 'under attack' myself also reduced, and the quantity of cups of tea required at three in the morning started to subside too.

As the nightmares and flashbacks begun to ease and PTSD wasn't ruling my existence the moments of bursting into tears when songs played on the radio (no idea why that triggered me) stopped again. The happy-go-lucky me was returning, and the music that plays in shops got my dancing shoes working again—and yes, I am one of those crazy women that do a little jig in public places (in fairness all my children and my granddaughter have inherited that from me).

PTSD had been ruling my existence and ruining my life and I'm determined this won't be happening again. The chaos within my mind cleared like the sun burning through mist but it took time without external help. I won't be taken down by someone else's actions next time and nor will I place myself in a position of being discarded again. I have come back stronger, and on my terms. I have also come back with the knowledge of the most qualified mind doctors in the country and in Europe who've had the mind to publish books.

It helps to have an extraordinary mind that thinks outside the box and never gives up on education, self-improvement or on hope.

Fighting back against adversity kept me going each day—it gave me purpose. Each small battle won was replaced with two new ones to face and on it went. Time after time I've felt downtrodden by surviving but each new dawn bought with it new faith and I had to hold onto that.

Before therapy with Gary, I never cried as that ability had been beaten out of me long before. During the tough times I've faced there's often a wish the waterworks could be turned off again, for once they begin there's no stopping them now. Once my eyes begin to leak the fountain of tears are relentless. Always leading to a feeling of depression and the realisation that I'm far from normal, it is at this point I'm most vulnerable and know however hard I try, however much work I put into recovery, someone or a situation I might be in will stop that occurring.

It seems the only people who fully understand me are those with the shared lived experiences or those who were there, standing beside me at the time. Sadly, or rightly, they are few in numbers.

Chapter Twelve

Kitchen Extensions (...from Kitchen Sagas)

One of my most popular chapters in *Lost Soul* was to share my post-brain cooking experiences in 'Kitchen Sagas.' Needless to say, my issues run far deeper. During the years of being stalked (same person or not) involved a series of house break-ins where, among other personal items, my saucepans and kitchen knives went missing. Sometimes things were returned under unusual circumstances—I'd find items in places that were designed to test my sanity. For example, I would return home to find a saucepan on my shed step in the back garden (even though the gate was high and locked from the inside). Once I returned late from work in the early hours of the morning on a weekend the children weren't home to find a dead bird attached to the back of my gate with one of my own knifes—I support anti-knife crime, and this runs deeper too. For anyone who has read my first trilogy, you might now be piecing together parts of my life that I've twisted into that fiction and understand my need to write. During these times, a truck was often (daily) parked outside our home while I cooked. I recognised it of course, but nobody was prepared to help and after repeatedly reporting it, just kept a diary and photographic evidence for it wasn't worth my time in making reports. Instead, I got on with living my life and hoped I'd survive.

Another incident—one that didn't occur in my home—left one of my children badly burnt. This occurred in a kitchen also, deemed an accident, but after being invited into the kitchen they then had a saucepan of boiling water and peas poured over their shoulder. Rather than cooling

73

the burn, it was dabbed with a dirty washing up sponge by someone who was first aid trained and left to fester.

A second kitchen accident occurred in that same household that cost another one of my children their two front teeth. They ran from one part of the house around a corner straight into someone carrying a plate of food from the other side of a breakfast bar. Luckily, they were infant teeth but far from ready to come out. The instant blood loss was substantial enough to ruin that plate of food and the teeth cut through the lip.

Another kitchen experience was when a hot water pipe burst in our bathroom. The first we knew of the situation was upon hearing the waterfall sounds as water cascaded onto the kitchen floor beneath it. There was no control over the temperature and no way of stopping the flow until the mains had been turned off. The tap for that was under the kitchen sink. Needless to say, in a house ran independently by a single mum that responsibility fell to me. The trip box was also in that room, which I felt, given the water was gushing through light fittings and plug sockets, deserved my attention first. Eventually I reached the mains tap but not before my whole body was soaked with water too hot to handle—but what choice did I have? Once water ceased flowing, I stood in approximately five inches of it.

My head injury occurred just over three years after my kitchen flooded. Bluntly put, is it any wonder given all the experiences before that date, is it no wonder I shut down. It was the event, however, that was catalyst to me fearing for my life in such an extreme manner that my memory vanished and from which my PTSD stemmed. When, during therapy, the sounds I could hear and the majority of smells I recall were those from the kitchen—which was the adjacent room—is it any wonder the kitchen remains the room in which I still struggle today. With all that happened surrounding this room buried deep within my subconscious, which wasn't revealed until months after my initial return home from hospital, is it any wonder I struggled to relearn with the effects of amnesia hindering progress in a room where so much difficulty had occurred. Not knowing what a knife, fork and spoons were called, or that spoons came in differing sizes are simple examples of how basic matters became. I'd make tea on the worktop, instead of in mugs and would become frustrated that there was a mess to clean without knowing how to do so and then replace the milk into the washing machine rather than the fridge.

During those early days, when it was taking me hours to relearn simple tasks, I was also prosecuting my employer. Under these circumstances it isn't uncommon to have a private investigator camp outside your home and take photographs. Distinctly remembering how uncomfortable I felt that there had been a vehicle parked outside for a considerable amount of time I ventured upstairs and fetched my professional camera. It wasn't charged, so thought if they were still there when it had enough to function, I'd attempt to catch them at their own game. Low and behold, from my hallway window (despite not being able to see through the viewfinder because of my poor eyesight) I could make out a camera pointing in my direction. I snuck out my front door, and under the protection from the shrubs in my front garden, gained a good view of the vehicle and took some wicked photographs of the vehicle and driver with his camera pointing right at me. I also went back indoors and did the same from my kitchen window—he obviously saw this happening and drove off but not before I'd photographed him and the precise direction of his camera's angle.

Nobody should underestimate my capability or indeed the tools I have at my disposal. I'd been a professional photographer a few years previous and although there was no longer the capability to manually focus the camera it has automatic features too. From all those years of being stalked and watched through my kitchen window, something triggered my hypervigilance about the man in this vehicle. Some might call it paranoia—I call it instinct for survival.

Life has moved forward from those days, thankfully. Struggling still occurs unless I occupy the kitchen space alone, the only times I have daytime flashbacks are in the kitchen when I'm distracted by something I'm not expecting. That said, I'm far from the dark days of hiding under the table, with much more control over regaining the here and now. It does make me a little 'snappy' out of frustration as I struggle to hold back my emotions as guilt engulfs me.

Chapter Thirteen

The Science: Brain Response to Trauma & Pain

Understanding how trauma affects your brain is a vital factor in recovery. Our natural reaction to life-threatening situations, the freeze-fight-flight response, is normal. It is how species survive and in psychological terms can be described through Charles Darwin's theory of evolution in which he states that evolution happens by natural selection. Individuals in a species show variation in physical characteristics and that those best suited to their environment are more likely to survive, finding food, avoiding predators, and resisting disease.

Our emotional response to trauma is determined by the amygdala, a small but vital part of the brain. Triggering powerful stress hormones and the nervous system responses that cause sweating, trembling, a racing heart, and elevated blood pressure—all normal responses that are potentially lifesaving if you are involved, for example, in a car crash.

However, your life would become a frenzy with your mind going into overdrive each time you heard a speeding car or the sound of brakes if your responses are triggered each time. Finding yourself caught up in this raging cycle would suddenly begin to feel unbearable and you would feel chronically scared. This is how PTSD manifests.

Chapter Fourteen

My Personal Pain

By now you know the cause of my injuries were by assault rather than a car accident, and that due to the nerve damage inside my brain resulting from that, I live with several residing issues. Pain, unfortunately, is a cross I bear. Discomfort always presents in the background, daily, although this is something I've learnt to dismiss a little like 'white noise' all these years on. Just a part of my life that's become a characteristic of who I've become—a part of my new identity. Coping with severe head pain was the most I needed to deal with initially and over the years I've learnt to cope with what is comparable to migraine pains. What would normally put folk in a dark room, incapacitated, I work through. My choice is to work it off in a day or suffer for a week and that's become my preference as the alternative would be to allow life to pass me by.

More recently I've suffered associated nerve damage affecting my spine, pain that is constant—some days are excruciating and others more bearable. Again, I find it easier if I'm able to work through this pain, but it doesn't leave room for the times of normal pain in other areas of my body such as tapping an elbow on a door frame or hitting my head. Such instances tip me over the edge of what my body can cope with. The back pain has increased due to my kidney stone issues and lessens when I've none passing which is a blessing.

Unfortunately, I'm unable to take pain relief: many asthmatics are not able to take ibuprofen (including me) and paracetamol, gives me seriously bad diarrhoea which is an intolerance built up from the cocktail of medications I now take. When my pain level reaches levels that would have most people calling an ambulance, those around me might notice me becoming slightly intolerant. This is especially noticeable if they constantly complain about minor ailments. I'm filled with empathy, don't get me wrong, but I internalise my suffering most of the time and as you will read in the chapter 'Limbic System,' I'm often at the tipping point from hearing about other people's issues which doesn't help when I then have to respond to anything 'extra' in my own life.

Although the chronic pain episodes have reduced, especially the pain that occurs inside my head from daily to an average of twice per month, my head does ache very mildly most days. On the days it doesn't hurt at all, a light-headedness feeling that's almost euphoric, takes over as if I've been given the strongest opiates. The high is incredible. Yet codeine is what's required to solve my spine pain issues these days. My issue with taking codeine is my mind has to be in its strongest position in order to cope with the drug in the first place—any sign of depression before taking it and I'm doomed. One tablet is enough to plunge me deeper into the darkness, and to cause hallucinations (and I'm difficult to handle when that happens)! Coping with the pain, then, is my better option, and probably the better option for Dave as hallucinations during depression are gloomy and really not funny like the ones I had in hospital on morphine.

Cracking on with the day, week, month, year—my life—has been the only way forward for me. As I've started to explain, my pain isn't isolated to my head. The nerve damage to my brain causes seizures (which do begin in my brain) and when they aren't controlled, they manifest into injury on top of the other complaints. We are talking molar teeth broken in half that have had to be extracted, a tendon in my thigh torn so badly it could be picked up externally and moved about, an old shoulder injury re-torn so severely it required a hydrocortisone injection before it healed, hydrocortisone in my hip when another seizure caused further issues to my mended tendon… and the list continues.

At times one or the other hands, or feet, are numb or have sharp shooting pains running through the digits, the length of my spine so sore that movement of any kind sends hot needles surging along it and my arms and legs. During what can only be described as 'neurological flair ups,' I cannot tell the difference between hot or cold water and have to place my trust in familiar settings on taps and showers. The injury I was supposed to heal from in three weeks—the mild concussion originally diagnosed—still gives me the most excruciating and complex pain eight years post trauma.

In Accident and Emergency departments, the surgeons you come across ask you to score the pain you're in out of ten, from your personal experience—ten being the worse pain imaginable. Kidney stones passing is my ten (documented to be the worse pain either a man or woman can experience). Asked to compare this to my historic pain, I've now moved the human bite—thankfully, a rare occurrence—which I now place at eight in evaluation as that pain had been short-lived. Next is my head pain. Although this lasted years, and the pain level reached was excruciating at times which did include nausea, I can honestly say upon reflection, it never reached the point of either of my top two. Then my thigh at six. Loosing teeth, five. My broken shoulder, collar bones, breast plate and multiple ribs are down at four. I've had other broken bones that take up the lower numbers. My spine pain sits at an eight most days, so when other pain tips me to a nine, I tend to venture to hospital because that's a safe environment for me to be medicated.

My new reality is that my body has become so accustomed to passing kidney stones, that I no longer take time off work to do so. When I'm injected or have bloods taken and there's no flinch, or I watch and the person doing the procedure is surprised at my non-reaction, that's because I cannot feel it. I've watched a lump being removed from my breast by a plastic surgeon under local anaesthetic (for which he called me mercenary). It took me an age and some serious persuading for him to allow this as he thought I'd pass out at the sight of my flesh protruding from the slit in my skin—that it would trigger my pain response. He was wrong. The whole process was fascinating, and I'd watch again!

My tolerance to pain is too high for I've experienced too much which does place me at risk at times. If you ever hear the words "I think I need to go to hospital," then I am in an emergency situation. More than likely hospital was required a minimum of three days previously (possibly three weeks ago). My nerve damage at its worse, when my spine feels like it's got hot needles passing along it, when it has lasted six relentless months alongside kidney pain is getting close to my tolerance level—the constant nauseous feeling is there but I can manage the sickness by taking controlling breaths. Normal, over the counter pain relief doesn't work for nerve damage and is out of the question for me anyhow because of the combination of asthma and my anti-convulsant medications. Coping is my only choice and that usually means working hard and placing my body through boundaries most would stumble at. What works for me wouldn't necessarily be the answer for somebody else. When I physically cannot move, I write and that works for me also.

Until recently the only solace had been that the more years that passed the more healing the nerve damage inside my head seemed to generate. In turn, the less effect this had on my body. The seizures had been controlled (with the help of medications), and the nerve damage didn't spread beyond my brain. Unfortunately, in more recent times, the relapses have been more severe and the price I pay for surviving and not living a stress-free life, bites me on the derriere.

Sometimes it feels like I'm running away from the journey.

Pain

Ripping through your body, like a hot blade,
Nothing will stop me, until I'm ready to fade.
I'll encompass all you are, until I'm gone,
Stopping you, despite your need to carry on.

I'm physical, you feel me when you rest,
Or upon movement, I will manifest.
I'm with you constantly, night and day,
During work, or when it's time for play.

Whatever's on your mind, I'll embrace that too,
There are limits to how I might affect you.
I'll sweep in and swipe you hard and fast,
And can't tell you how long I will last.

Chapter Fifteen

Stress Hormones

Ignoring stress causes harm, so it makes sense to learn from past mistakes. Suppressing inner cries for help most definitely doesn't suppress stress hormones—in matter of fact it enhances their production. Stress hormones produce symptoms that demand your attention, creating a link between physical sensations and emotions. One way or another stress will manifest itself either psychologically or through pain, disease, or injury. This process might take a few weeks, or months, but rest assured, something will develop.

Change occurs through becoming aware of your sensations and how your body interacts with the world around you. Being physically self-aware is step one in releasing the past. Noticing the difference between and being able to describe your bodily feelings of the sensations beneath the emotions you are feeling is a huge step towards recovery. For example: the pressure, heat, tension, tingling, and feeling hollow sensations that can be associated with anger or fear will go a long way in giving you indication that your body is sensing anxiety when your mind has not caught up with processing that fact. This will give you time to ground yourself before the negative emotions begin to take over and will allow you to continue with your routine.

During relaxation you are able to become aware of your breathing, bodily gestures, and movements and in time subtle differences become apparent between relaxed and heightened states.

Let's link chronic pain and stress, as those of us who suffer both know that we tend to have pain flares when stress is a factor in our lives. Sometimes we might be sensitive in acknowledging this fact vocally in fear that others perceive our pain is in fact 'all in our head.' With regards to stress not causing nerve damage, this is true. There's a huge but here. Stress does cause inflammation and that, in turn can have a catastrophic effect on our lives. Inflammation of already damaged nerves causes extreme pain. Stress also makes other pain worse and has a significant role in the production of pain (for me, stress causes the left side of my face to swell—I look as if I've had a stroke but is, instead, swollen nerves). The development of pain itself, from acute injuries or illness to long-term maintenance of chronic pain, has everything to do with stress response—thus if it were not for a stress response, we wouldn't have pain as we know it.

Chapter Sixteen

Pain Signals

Pain is registered through microscopic pain receptors called nociceptors in your skin (each form one end of a nerve cell (neurone) that is connected to the other end in the spinal cord by a long nerve fibre or axon. When a receptor is activated it sends an electrical signal along the nerve fibre, which is bundled with many others to form a peripheral nerve. The electrical signal passes along the neurone within the peripheral nerve to reach the spinal cord in the neck to the dorsal horn, where they are transmitted from one neurone to another at junctions (synapses). This is done by means of chemical messengers (neurotransmitters) before the signal is passed further along the spinal cord and into the brain.

Inside the brain the signal reaches the thalamus, which is a sorting station that relays signals to different parts of the brain. From here your pain signal will then travel to the somatosensory cortex (which is responsible for physical sensation), to the frontal cortex (in charge of thinking) and the limbic system (which is linked to emotions). This process will result in you feeling the sensation of pain in whichever part of your body you have hurt—it's what makes you say "ouch" or think "what was that?" or to say a profanity under your breath, or louder (I say "bollocks"). It also allows you to react emotionally, for example you might feel annoyed, irritated, or upset—you might cry for example.

Often you will have reacted involuntarily before being consciously aware of your injury. This is the case for pain that is sudden or strong and is called a reflex response. Such instances occur in your spinal cord—motor neurones activate, contracting the necessary muscles to move you away from the source of what might be harming you. Occurring within a fraction of a second, before the signal has been relayed to your brain. In some instances, you would have removed yourself from what is harming you before becoming conscious of the pain itself.

Chapter Seventeen

Linking Stress and Pain

Given this book is specific to PTSD I will be concentrating on how stress and pain are related and how the stress response can lead to pain or make existing pain (through inflammation) which makes existing pain worse.

Our immune system is our natural defence system, which works in conjunction with our nervous system and our endocrine (hormone) system. Although these systems are categorised as different bodily systems, they work simultaneously, functioning in harmony. We do need to note that while we are talking about the immune system the following structures within the brain: the nervous system, neurotransmitters, and hormones are also functioning in order that the immune system functions.

Playing the role of defence in response to injury or infection, the immune system produces inflammation, which is a catch-all term describing various chemical messengers and cells designed to fight infection or prepare for healing—this is what makes us sick when we are fighting viral or bacterial infections, for example.

Scientific study in both psychology and biology have allowed us to know that inflammation plays a role in mood changes and behaviour—both of which can allow us to fight off infection or respond to injury that allows for damage control. These psychological responses are also responses to danger. In discovering that the immune system is part of a three-way response with the nervous system and the endocrine system has gone a long way in understanding the fight-flight-freeze reaction—what is known bodily as the stress response. It is our cognitive, emotional, motivational, bodily, behavioural, and social response to either a danger, or what we might more generically call a 'stressor.'

Stressors from trauma (and I'll use the physical assault and resultant injuries on myself as an example) cause automatic reactions without conscious awareness or intention due to our natural in-built stress response. This quick review of the multifaceted (biopsychosocial) aspects of this stress response shows us what would normally happen (and in brackets I share my reaction as my training forced a different response from me that contributed to what I now go through):

Our cognitive response becomes heightened as we focus on the danger—we learn about our circumstances and subsequent acute memory of the stressor. Our emotional response is also heightened and alarmed. Anger and/or fear are increased along with an increased sense of social belonging. Our motivational response is heightened to drive to react to protect yourself (for me I wasn't allowed to fight back but trained to restrain professionally without harming the other person—my motivational response was to deescalate the situation which takes patience and calmness demanding control despite being under attack). The body response includes increased muscle tension, heart rate, blood pressure, increased glucose in the bloodstream and an increased immune response (but for me I was trained to remain calm, forcing my heartrate back down to normal and my muscles to relax). The behavioural and social response—the fight, flight, freeze response and tend-and-befriend behaviours are different for each of us in any given situation. This is designed for us to perform better and to survive situations in order that our species might survive. (Turning my back on the situation I found myself in and to have walked away—flight—would have resulted in death, of that I'm certain. My attack was extended because colleagues were sent to the wrong room, and I thus faced danger alone and as a result I disassociated. This was also a huge risk, which could have resulted in death, had I not pulled myself together as fast as I did. I couldn't legally fight either as I've already explained. I wanted to run and couldn't so froze momentarily. The other natural reaction is fight and that wasn't permitted).

My situation was, therefore, a combination of all responses as panic had set in and then a sense of 'control' as I took the situation in hand and regained dominance over the person attacking because of their psychosis. There was no 'fight' but instead professionalism as I came to terms with the devastating situation I'd been left facing alone and regained my purpose. My stress response had been replaced with my 'calm response' and a conscious decision to live—I'd gone against all natural built-in response systems designed for survival in an extreme situation.

I couldn't feel the pain until afterwards, while awaiting my colleagues to take over from me.

Our immune system, then operates on a large scale, its defensive function part of a greater whole protecting our stress response. In turn, our stress response is a whole contingent of automatic responses from the microscopic to the macroscopic. From here, we can also see how the stress response is a whole contingent of automatic responses, which occurs when we are threatened by danger. In other words, it is the stress that the human organism undergoes when threatened.

Second, we see that in our society we tend to categorize these microscopic to macroscopic responses under particular headings, such as those that are biological, those that are psychological, and those that are social. We subsequently tend to think that these categories represent actually different things and then begin to wonder how they are connected. However, these categories do not represent distinct kinds of things. They are heuristic categories that reflect different aspects of the same kind of thing, the human organism, or person. In this way, we no longer wonder how "the mind" is connected to "the body," as if they are two separate kinds of matters. Vitally, we consider that our body and mind are one entity: that cognitive, emotional, motivational, and social aspects of the stress response occur simultaneously with biological aspects of stress responses—that they occur within a 'person' rather than a 'mind' or a 'body.' This is where the term biopsychosocial stems from in order that scientists and healthcare providers don't make the distinction between the mind and body when discussing this subject.

Chapter Eighteen

Inflammation

Many natural, automatic responses are involved alongside the stress response. One of those is the immune system, which kicks into a high gear to produce inflammation, which makes sense when you think about it. If our immune system is functioning in 'high gear' as it fights off infection from scratches, or bites, it prevents nasty bacteria taking hold and spreading further into our body.

Again, this is a triage of systems working simultaneously and this peak performance results from the immune system working in conjunction with the sympathetic nervous system and the endocrine system. During the fight or flight response differing brain structures send messages via a highway of nerves to the pituitary and adrenal glands, which then produce hormones such as cortisol and adrenaline (also known as epinephrine). These chemicals are often called 'stress hormones' and they are responsible for getting us hyped. Cortisol prevents insulin (another hormone produced in the pancreas) from working which means glucose increases in the bloodstream—giving increased energy. These hormones trigger the immune response in the form of white blood cells and what are called cytokines. We call this immune system response 'inflammation.'

Inflammation, by definition is when the injury area becomes red, swollen, and sensitive to the touch. It shows that our immune system works and that the white blood cells and cytokines are engaging in their protective function in damage control. The sensitivity you feel is present because the immune response irritates the nerves in the area, serving as a protective function preventing us from poking and thus re-injuring the area. Subsequently, we are motivated to protect or guard the area.

Chapter Nineteen

Immediate Hormone Response in the Brain

Cytokines are also present in the brain at this point, intermingling with hormones and neurotransmitters. If the injury or infection is severe enough or widespread enough, this mix of chemicals in our nervous system, including the brain, can lead to a feeling of being 'run-down' which is better known as 'malaise' or 'fatigue.' It is at this point we are often motivated to rely on/depend upon others for help and then feel upset and abandoned when they ignore us or do not notice this need—this is particularly dominant for those with PTSD.

After the threat passes and the infection and injuries have been successfully fought, and healed, cortisol informs the brain to begin turning off the stress response. This multifaceted process—from the beginning of the chapters 'Brain Response' to 'Trauma and Pain' through to this moment is remarkable—we are built to survive in the most elegant way to optimise our chances of survival when threatened by danger.

Of course, this system evolved to survive attacks from lions, invasions from Vikings etc. More commonly we face psychological and social threats these days. These might be the death of a spouse, child or another family member or, perhaps a close friend; a job loss and subsequent loss of income that accompanies it; critical bosses and bullying in the workplace; discrimination; a family member joining the armed forces and going to war or experiences of war yourself; a family member, or yourself with terminal illness; a traumatic event… the list is endless, but they are threats to our livelihood and well-being that we are hard-wired to respond to, by releasing our stress response.

Moreover, our minds have the ability to anticipate psychological and social threats—the threats listed above are not the only commonly faced threats that can trigger stressors or have potential for anticipating anxiety, which is the worrying or ruminating about the possibility of threats.

Chapter Twenty

Stress and Inflammation

Us humans have an amazing capacity to worry. Let's face it, everything that could go wrong, does on occasion, which is a form of the stress response prepping us for danger. It becomes an issue, however when the stress response is stuck in the 'on' position and we constantly prepare for danger when there's only a possibility of one or no actual threat of it occurring.

Often, for example, there are situations that cannot be avoided, and I find myself in a position of being involved in conversation on difficult subjects. In such instances, I place time restrictions upon them for the sake of my own sanity. After all, I am only human and not a robot capable of turning off chemical reactions to stress. With my own mental well-being to consider and that of my physical health too, I believe this to be the only way forward without leading a solitary life. For without conscious intention our body will respond with the stress response whether we are actually living through a stressor or perceiving there might be one in the future. Either way, with stress and inflammation making pain worse, those of us who live with chronic pain conditions will already know that this type of stress can have the potential to make pain unbearable.

Experiencing stressful events or worrying about the possibility of such events will trigger your immune system in conjunction with your nervous system and endocrine system putting our inflammation in response to the real or perceived threat, in turn causing irritation to nerves (which includes the nerves in the area of your chronic pain). Sensitivity results, which is the desired effect under normal circumstances. Due to these nerves being more sensitive to begin with, they require less stimuli to cause increased discomfort. This is your immune system working efficiently to do exactly what it was designed to do under threat. While this is problematic, it is normal and common.

Unresolved stress that lasts a length of time becomes increasingly challenging, with the stress response continuing unabated. The level of inflammation becomes higher and higher, with the nervous system becoming sensitised. This results in widespread inflammation, increased and widespread pain in the form of body aches and the feeling of 'malaise' or 'fatigue' as mentioned before. Additionally, these higher levels of pain can lead to you feeling as if you've got flu without the other flu symptoms.

This is where the tend-and-befriend aspect of the stress response enters your needs. If you're not cared for at this point you will feel abandoned as your need for others increases. You now require comfort and care and don't want to be alone. If you are alone, this adds insult to injury for it's a natural defence strategy.

In order to reduce chronic pain, there are therapeutic pain management techniques that can be taught through rehabilitation programmes. This reduces the stress response in the presence of pain, reducing the reactivity of the nervous system, teaching you how to maintain reduced reactivity of your nervous system which leads to less inflammation, less pain, greater energy, and motivation. Furthermore, it will lead to greater abilities to independently lead a more fulfilled life. The Institute for Chronic Pain has a number of resources that provide information on chronic pain rehabilitation—but ultimately the choice is yours—as the patient—on how you approach your pain and how you learn to cope and deal with it as to the outcome that arises, rather than what your healthcare provider can do for you.

In other words, hope lies within you for healing.

Chapter Twenty-One

Limbic system

During my preface, I mentioned the limbic system in passing. This complicated system involves several areas of the brain. When my PTSD strikes, I have the complexity that I'm also fighting brain trauma from the residual damage caused by the assault. Stress placed on the limbic system is enough to cause memory issues, but I already face these—I readily walk past close family members in the street even when I know I'm meeting up with them (and we are talking about my own children here) because facial recognition is something I personally struggle with, even though we are post eight years after the attack! Relearning this information has also given insight into why I struggle to use my conventional memory while coping with complex PTSD. Nor is it lost on me that because my limbic system often fails, I now have a lifetime of anti-convulsant medications to look forward to in conjunction with the residing nerve damage from the assault.

Not wanting to blind you with the science which, ironically, I do understand and have studied from therapeutic, psychological, and criminological perspectives I have outlined the important factors of how the limbic system performs (or doesn't).

Also known as the paleomammalian cortex, the limbic system is a set of brain structures located on both sides of the thalamus immediately beneath the medial temporal lobe of the cerebrum, primarily in the forebrain. Supporting various functions that include emotion, behaviour, long-term memory, and olfaction (smell), this is the area of the brain that emotional life is largely housed and where the formation of memories occurs. Its primitive structure means that the limbic system is involved in lower order emotional processing from other sensory systems and consists of the amygdala, mammillary bodies, stria medullaris, central gray, and dorsal and ventral nuclei of gudden.

Processed information is relayed to a collection of structures including from the telencephalon, diencephalon, and mesencephalon, including the prefrontal cortex, cingulate gyrus, limbic thalamus, hippocampus including the parahippocampal gyrus and subiculum, nucleus accumbens (limbic striatum), anterior hypothalamus, ventral tegmental area, midbrain raphe nuclei, habenular commissure, entorhinal cortex, and olfactory bulbs.

That's a lot of information, so is it any wonder that, when this system fails during episodes of PTSD, we crash land? Although the limbic system isn't considered an isolated entity responsible for neurological regulation of emotion, it is certainly part of the process responsible for memory and other interacting areas such as motivation, emotion, and learning. It is where the subcortical structures meet the cerebral cortex.

Additionally, it is also the system that operates the endocrine system and the autonomic nervous system, being highly interconnected with the nucleus accumbens, which plays a role in sexual arousal and the 'high' derived from certain recreational drugs. Responses such as these are heavily modulated by dopaminergic projections from the limbic system.

The basal ganglia are a set of subcortical structures that direct intentional movements, which are located near the thalamus and hypothalamus, receiving input from the cerebral cortex, which sends outputs to the motor centres in the brain stem. Part of the basal ganglia, called the striatum, controls posture and movement. If there is inadequate supply of dopamine in the striatum, this can lead to symptoms of Parkinson's disease—dopamine is produced in several areas of the brain including the substantia nigra and ventral tegmental areas. It is a neurohormone released by the hypothalamus and is an inhibitor or prolactin release from the anterior lobe of the pituitary.

The limbic system is also tightly connected to the prefrontal cortex, a connection related to the pleasure obtained from problem solving. In the past this connection was surgically severed in order to 'cure' emotional disorders—a psychosurgery procedure called prefrontal lobotomy—the results of which often meant patients became passive and lacking in motivation.

The limbic system isn't a structure but a network if interactions within the cerebral cortex. These interactions are closely linked to olfaction, emotions, drives, autonomic regulation, memory and pathologically to encephalopathy, epilepsy, psychotic symptoms, and cognitive defects. The functional relevance of the limbic system has proven to serve many different functions such as affects/emotions, memory, sensory processing, time perception, attention, consciousness, instincts, autonomic/vegetative control, and actions/motor behaviour. Some of the disorders associated with the limbic system and its interacting components are epilepsy and schizophrenia.

The hippocampus is also an important aspect of our brains involved with various processes relating to cognition and is one of the most well understood and heavily involved limbic interacting structures. For me, learning about spatial memory has given an understanding on why I've found it so difficult to use my memory palace to establish 'when' while retrieving memories.

Spatial memory has many sub-regions in the hippocampus and is where adults and adolescents generate new neurons (adult-born granules). These new neurons contribute to pattern separation in spatial memory, increasing the firing in cell networks which causes stronger memory formations. This is thought to integrate spatial and episodic memories with the limbic system via feedback loop that provides emotional context of a particular sensory input. All this happens in the dorsal hippocampus, on the right.

The left hippocampus is the recall of 'what,' 'when' and 'where' of each of our experiences to compose the retrieved memory and is also a key component in learning. The hippocampus, as a result of training through new learning, produces an upsurge of new neurons and neural circuits which causes an overall improvement in learning new tasks. This neurogenesis contributes to the creation of adult-born granules cells (GC). The creation of these cells exhibited "enhanced excitability" in the dentate gyrus (DG) of the dorsal hippocampus, impacting the hippocampus and its contribution to the learning process.

Damage to the hippocampus region of the brain effects cognitive functioning—particularly memory and especially spatial memory. Such damage may result from brain injuries. Researchers have a particular interest in and have investigated the effects that high emotional arousal and certain types of drugs had on the recall ability in this specific memory type. Studies reinforcing the impact that the hippocampus has on memory processing, in particular the recall function of spatial memory that have involved stressed situations have proven memory implications. Furthermore, impairment to the hippocampus can occur from prolonged exposure to stress hormones such as glucocorticoids (GCs), which target the hippocampus and cause disruption in explicit memory.

The amygdala is another integrative (and the deepest) part of the limbic system. This part of the brain is involved in many cognitive processes and is considered the most primordial and vital part of the limbic system. Also impacting memory, this time the semantic division of episodic-autobiographical memory (EAM) networks. It encodes, stores, and retrieves EAM memories. The amygdala's main function is to charge cues so that mnemonic events of a specific emotional significance can be successfully searched within the appropriate neural nets and re-activated. These cues for emotional events created by the amygdala encompass the EAM networks previously mentioned.

Additional to memory, the amygdala is important to attention and emotional processes. In cognitive terms, attention is the ability to focus on some stimuli while ignoring others. A deficit in functionality can lead to mental illness such as anxiety disorders.

Social processing, such as the evaluation of faces in social processing is an area of cognition specific to the amygdala. It's also the area of the brain that allows evaluation of the trustworthiness of an individual, and that in damaged individuals trust and betrayal can become confused, and that trust can easily be placed in someone who has done them wrong. First impressions also become more difficult for someone who has damaged this part of their brain.

Chapter Twenty-Two

Substance P

Substance P is composed of a chain of eleven amino acid residues and is a member of the tachykinin neuropeptide family. Acting as a neurotransmitter and a neuromodulator Substance P is produced from a polyprotein precursor. Released from the terminals of specific sensory nerves, Substance P is found in the brain and spinal cord and is associated with inflammatory processes and pain.

Imbalances between the neurotransmitters serotonin and substance P has been linked to PTSD—the greater the imbalance the more serious the symptoms. It is now believed that those of us suffering with PTSD have altered brain anatomy and function which is providing evidence for speculation that the biological basis for psychiatric disorders includes a shift in the balance between different signalling systems in the brain. This information has been proven through the use of sophistical positron emission tomography (PET) scanners in Sweden. Rather than the degree of change in a single system it found imbalance between systems which could be used to design improved pharmacological treatments.

Presently, PTSD is routinely treated with selective serotonin reuptake inhibitors (SSRIs) which have direct effects on the serotonin system. Although these drugs provide relief for many, they don't help everyone. Through the research mentioned above, restoring the balance between the serotonin and substance P systems could be the way forward in treating those of us suffering as a result of traumatic incidents.

Given that chronic stress places our health at risk, and places havoc on our minds and bodies we must take back control. This is a difficult task when we are hard-wired to react to stress in ways to protect ourselves against threats from predators and aggressors.

Chapter Twenty-Three

Loneliness

Often we don't admit to such emotional and social needs as requiring togetherness, for we live in a society where strength matters. I've mentioned this feeling a couple of times and thus feel it deserves a few words separate from the other text, and a dedicated chapter.

Despite being among those I love dearly there are often times of extreme loneliness felt for varying reasons. Perhaps lack of understanding, being misunderstood or knowing that what might be going through my mind at any given time hasn't ever been through theirs (not that I'd wish my past on anyone). I've hinted at a life I've lived, yet many of my personal experiences have never been voiced or written about—that's my harsh reality—my burden that often weighs me down. That I don't burden others is, I believe, why my depression exists and persists.

Recognition is important, as is remembering that social and emotional needs have been with us from the beginning of man and to need interaction isn't being weak—this is your stress response doing exactly what it has been designed to do in order for you to guard yourself against the threat of your own well-being. Above I mention this need is higher within those suffering from PTSD. A deep feeling of loneliness has a pernicious effect on mental health which is likely to have a bidirectional relationship with psychopathology.

Loneliness is a distressing psychological experience occurring when an individual feels their social connectedness is insufficient—for example it lacks or is absent of intimate relationships or close attachments or that there is a lack of desire to have a wider engaging social network that would provide a sense of belonging and companionship.

Traumatic 'aloneness' has a deeper layer attached still. Often it can stem from childhood, but not always. I know exactly where mine stems from—I was thirty-one years old. Let's describe it as a hole that is supposed to be filled with love and to make you feel important (at whatever age that might be). This black hole that consumes you can now never be fully filled, not completely: not today, nor tomorrow. You might be sitting with family feeling a sensation that might be interpreted as hunger that food can't fix (not even chocolate). Alcohol doesn't work either. Recognising it exists helps, healing from it through therapy goes some way towards repairing this hole and in making it considerably smaller.

Recognition, being heard, and being nurtured all contribute to the connectedness and closeness we need to survive once more and allow us to love ourselves as well as others. Yes, I said 'ourselves'—at my lowest, when my self-esteem is non-existent, I loathe the skin I'm in and I know that anyone who has experienced what I have has, at some point probably gone through this too. It goes a long way, then, in enabling survivors of man-made traumas (those often left with a lasting sense of terror, horror, endangerment, and betrayal) in beginning to relate to others by letting their guard down again and relearning how to trust once more. When events occur that place doubt in this trust, however small they might seem to others, it triggers the stress response once more.

New relationships, as a result of long-lasting trauma, can feel scary or dangerous to a trauma survivor in the beginning or when changes occur within that relationship. The smallest of niggles trigger reminders casting doubt—for which I've created a process I go through bringing me back to reality!

Additionally, anxiety attached to PTSD can also make you feel isolated and detached from those you love which is a disconcerting feeling. This adds to the guilt, self-loathing and all the other negative emotions you already have—the abyss deepens each time I fall into it, and it's getting more difficult to claw my way back out.

Acknowledging it is perfectly okay.

Chapter Twenty-Four

Living with Anxiety & Flashbacks

During the end of twenty-twenty and into twenty-one, as I laid in the darkness of night (as awake as I might have been during the daytime) my anxiety was rife. Thoughts ran through my mind conjuring up 'what if's.' Scenarios heightened my mind, and more often than not they were the type that if they were to become reality, it would have meant danger was imminent. Anyone reading this might think I've been diagnosed with an anxiety disorder, other than anxiety attached to PTSD. Yet I've not. My reality is astonishingly different and what might appear to most as anxiety is, in point of fact, a lost memory returning—the majority of the time. After my head injury in twenty-fourteen I lost my memory and recalling my past has proven difficult. Much of it did return, but there is still a long way to go before all of my past has been reclaimed.

Through correspondence, past journaling and legal documentation I am generally able to justify what my brain is trying to tell me—I can normally prove to myself that what I am 'worrying' about during my awake hours in the night is actually not anxiety, although it releases the same chemical reaction in my brain and body as anxiety would—the stress response is exactly the same either way. As we've already discovered the release of chemicals occurs even if no real threat is present and mine are triggered by my past catching up with me in this manner.

Occasionally anxiety presents itself as actual anxiety, but that's not necessarily been without justification. My mind has, in some circumstances, run away with itself and I've written my thoughts down (which I no longer do). More often than not these thoughts have manifested into the truth (this is a rare phenomenon in all honesty, with research showing that only 1% of anxiety manifests into actual events). We do need to consider that I have also studied human behaviour, thus when you are dealing with someone who is following the same pattern of behaviour that another person from your past had done, despite that having been years ago, behaviour patterns are easy to predict. A scenario that proved unhelpful to me retaining a sense of calm within me.

Despite it being easy to control thought processes during daylight hours (during the times I had control of my conscious thoughts), that isn't so easy following severe nightmares when the stress response is triggered during the night. Living through six years of stalking taught me to think ahead, to predict, and to be a step ahead. Unfortunately, it created an anxious mind at the time, too. People can be predictable and when you become heightened your mind is vigilant—this serves to protect you and enables survival. Unfortunately, it also ensures that my stress response is triggered far too easily.

During the height of my anxiety last time around, I had to stop writing my thrillers. Previously writing had helped calm my senses and for me to overcome but I'd been working on a novel called *At Risk*, in which I was incorporating some aspects of my stalking story into the fiction. Despite all locations being changed and the characters having a massive makeover, the whole process became far too much. Within our private lives certain aspects of the psychological side of my manuscript were beginning to shadow what was now devastating me in the here and now. It was at this point I decided to begin journaling again, knowing I wanted to write about PTSD in the future and the complexities of living with and around the condition. From that, this book was born—which is exactly how *Lost Soul* was created too.

I hope I've dug deep enough.

Avoiding stress as much as humanly possible is important to each of us, although given our hectic lives I appreciate that's not always doable. For me, it's vital. Not only is stress a trigger for seizures (which I obviously need to avoid like the plague), but it also plays havoc with PTSD too. Triggering stress hormones for those with epilepsy or seizure disorders and or PTSD not only makes us vulnerable to the symptoms of those complex disorders but for me personally, the lack of sleep that arrives with stress and anxiety can also be a trigger for my seizures. Sleep deprivation alone is enough to trigger the 'smaller' episodes and when your body is physically tired there is also the vulnerability to external infections that might be around, such as colds to consider. Infection is, unfortunately, a trigger for tonic clonic seizures in my case.

When external stress is being placed on family life with the intension of causing havoc within the home, that places immense pressure upon everyone. Despite being a great believer in owning how you react to such situations, being at the receiving end of constant tension while dealing with my own complex health issues became too much. As well as dealing with everyone else's anxieties on top of my own, I actually felt I'd nobody to turn to for help myself—my head was ready to explode and of course it did so, with a chemical release.

Life that is spiralling out of control, for me, means unwanted memories returning to my nights and for threatful, broken sleep patterns interfering with my well-being. In turn the quality of my life took a sharp U-turn for the worse and peacefulness was replaced with terror—

flashbacks re-occurred, and the cycle of doom that I'd left behind re-commenced. Suppressing my emotion followed, for I didn't want to admit to my family that it was happening all over again. Feelings of guilt, of failure and that I had let everyone around me down (including myself) were overwhelming. This added to the anxiety, to self-doubt and to that feeling of falling deep into the abyss where I was drowning in sorrow.

During these times there's also this ultimate feeling of being watched. Granted this stems from all the years I was stalked and physically watched, but this is also a common factor in PTSD symptoms. When then, those around you start to notice your symptoms you feel judged. This is a negative cycle that only you feel and twist in your mind—and, of course, you perceive that if those close to you can see these changes, then it stands to reason that other folk from the outside world can do so too, and you convince yourself of this.

The curtains in our home come across with no intention of me opening them, and the mirrors come down for looking at my own reflection is no longer an option. Eisoptrophobia is a rare fear of looking at your reflection in a mirror and if my symptoms persisted constantly, I'd agree that this would be my issue. However, they don't. While my self-esteem is hitting rock bottom, I cannot fathom why anyone would want to look at me, take my photograph or see me on social media and so I save them the trouble and don't share myself while I'm feeling like this. As far as I'm concerned, I'm not the same person as before and this is reflective in the person that I see staring back at me in my reflection—so why on earth would I place myself in front of a mirror? For many years now, I've dried my hair without using one and applied face cream rather than make up. At my worse I've crumbled to the floor in floods of tears in front of a mirror and cannot see the point of having them around. When well, they don't bother me and hang on the walls, and I can once again face my reflection without issue.

Please remember that there have been four attackers in my life, each playing a role in the disabling effects that suffocate me through PTSD. The last believed I was the devil as they looked at me, they were seeking protection from me against him. During their episode of psychosis, it wasn't me they were attacking, but the demons their voices were telling them to. My poem *'Institutionalised'* that I shared in *Lost Soul* was about this situation and is as close as I can get to explaining the personality of the person who attacked me, from their perspective.

Avoiding stress is, then, paramount. Certainly, I wouldn't want to be living with me while I'm gripped with PTSD, for I don't like living with myself too much. On the flip side of that I'd be doing all in my power to ensure life ran smoothly in order that triggers were eliminated, as they are manageable, which makes the remainder of life easier to deal with when my symptoms do occur. To be jolted awake in the middle of the night by one of my nightmares is bad enough for me but for the other half it must be awful. He then has to endure the tears and no explanation as I won't discuss trauma in our bedroom. It is the room we retreat to relax at the end of the day and one in which there shouldn't be any negativity.

Again, it's the perfect excuse to avoid what I should be facing.

Again, avoidance is a common factor in PTSD. I've not returned to the place where I was attacked at work. I did return to where I was raped once, an experience one of my fiction characters will share one day. Let's just say, here and now, I didn't return a second time.

Once awake, the flashbacks commence, my eyes wide open. Like a film playing inside my head, sometimes fragmented but often in full detail, every moment relived as if I am back in the moment. Time flows as if its 'real-time,' an uninterrupted playthrough of the traumatic experience which includes every aspect of the pain felt, of the emotions, the sounds and how everything around me smelt. Every sensation makes me feel as if it's happening all over again, as if I'm back on location and not in my own bed. The only way to interrupt these scenes playing in my head is if I'm physically stopped by someone else and then I'm startled to such extreme that I retract from them frightened. It takes me several seconds to come around and to be able to respond.

I never reach the end of the scenes, I physically can't. For the memories are not complete—instead, they are fragmented and frustrated endings I cannot fathom until I sit at my desk and write in a journal and then compare my work to my diaries from ears ago. This is how I know that writing brings out my truth.

Ironically, during these times of crisis, I feel emotionally numb except for when I experience flashbacks, when every emotion of the trauma haunts me.

Determining what is real and what is not, which isn't always as easy as it might seem, is the difficult part. Not everything in my past could always be openly talked about with my children for I've protected them from so much. With that in mind, there were a select few people who were told a little of my past. Some of those people have now passed away. Dave knows what I've recalled but as time passes more is coming back—

even he is unaware of the finer details—I've not shared with him explicit details of individual scenarios during the nine years of trauma from being raped to the end of being stalked for example. He does know more than is in this book.

I'm unsure why the nights give me such a hard time other than they are long due to my insomnia. As the years passed after my head trauma this was put down to a fear of having seizures when I fell to sleep (the majority of my seizures do happen upon falling asleep). My mature studies took me into late nights as did my teen partying days and I'd still rather stay up late and rise late as I find it easier to sleep when most would be on their third cuppa. Ironically, most of my trauma happened during daylight hours (but not all). The one that I've had to keep zipped up inside me for so long for various reasons had the most effect for that very reason. There's another I'll be sharing in *At Risk* that happened at night, the scene has been transformed into a nightmare for the book, but I'll leave it there for you to read that at a later date.

Transparency

Anxiety rising like a tide pulled by the moon,
Compelling, all-encompassing. A mind gone too soon.
PTSD has its claws firmly into me,
Past events bringing me to my knees.

Hatred fills my heart, a self-loathing uncontrolled,
A desire to be loved, a need to have you hold.
Me tightly. The desire to be loveable,
In my own skin, to feel comfortable.

Mechanically I go about my routine,
Behind an invisible smoke screen.
That protects me from the vulnerability,
That the world places judgement upon me.

Everyone looks deep into my soul, so I perceive,
They see the demons lurking, I believe.
I live behind glass, my life on show,
My thoughts on display, for all to know.

Chapter Twenty-Five

Nightmares

Hyperarousal during sleep frequently occurs in conjunction with PTSD, playing a pivotal role in both the development and maintenance of the disorder. Eventually reduced sleep occurs that requires particular clinical attention. Nightmares often present themselves as exact replications or more symbolic representations of the traumatic experiences that have been experienced and usually occur during rapid eye movement sleep (REMS). Insomnia usually follows alongside a fear of sleep and a loss of control of having nightmares.

PTSD is also associated with obstructive sleep apnea (OSA), repeated OSA events lead to frequent oxygen desaturations and arousals. Repeated insomnia, nightmares and OSA may trigger and exacerbate each other which forms a vicious cycle. Additionally, periodic limb movement disorder (PLMD) in PTSD patients can be associated with arousals/awakenings as can periods of sleep paralysis (which is typical during REMS sleep-wake transitions) and are often accompanied by distressing experiences, referred to as hypnagogic or hypnopompic hallucinations. Although the exact frequency is unclear, PTSD is also linked to remarkable disruptive nocturnal behaviours, including abnormal vocalizations and complex body movements.

Research strongly indicates that disturbed sleep is not merely a symptom or consequence of PTSD, but constitutes an influencing, triggering and prolonging factor for it. Sleep disturbances prior to and/or shortly after trauma increase the risk for PTSD.

Sleep disturbances also affect the clinical course of PTSD—poor sleep quality is associated with reduced responsiveness to trauma-focused therapy whereas interventions targeting insomnia, nightmares or OSA improve sleep quality and as a result can improve daytime PTSD symptoms.

Common relations between sleep disturbances and PTSD suggest that disturbed sleep constitutes a casual factor in PTSD. This is partly based on sleep's role in memory consolidation and also memory regulation. Memory consolidation occurs during both slow wave sleep (SWS; deep non-REMS) and REMS. The processing of emotional memories is thought to happen primarily during REMS.

Traumatic memories arise due to, in part, a failure in extinction learning—learning that the previously conditioned stimulus no longer represents a threat. Thus, it is suggested that REMS disturbances, resulting from the noradrenergic hyperactivation typical of PTSD, hamper the consolidation of extinction memory, leading to a failure of the extinction memory to persist. Sleep disturbances following a traumatic event, including fragmented REMS, predict the development of PTSD. In order to make the bedroom a safe environment to aid sleep the following should be evaluated: eliminate all trauma-related triggers associated with sleep from the bedroom and ensure the room is adequately light or dark. In doing these two, what might seem small tasks, you can reduce hyperarousal levels.

Unfortunately, nightmares are at times prominent in my life. They are another way for my memories to return through PTSD and begin fragmented in the beginning. Nightly, they become clearer as the traumatic experience unfolds and clarity of the event is recovered. Once I'm awake (usually three or four in the morning) I'm done with sleep.

The price I pay for being me.

Chapter Twenty-Six

Adrenaline and Me

Emotional arousal was something I became addicted to. Adrenaline pumped through my veins daily during my thirties due to no fault of my own. Subjected to a lifestyle I hadn't wanted, one in which there was the need to be looking over my shoulder every day of my life my heart pumped a little faster than it should have each time there was a need to leave the house—more often than not while I was inside it too. You've already read a little on the nine years of trauma endured so let's focus on how the six years of being stalked affected me at the time.

Being stalked is a scary concept. It's about inducing fear [in my case] because they were rejected and perceived that as an insult. They felt wounded and were seeking vindication. There are other scenarios why stalking commences (but I knew mine). Receiving phone calls, often numerous times per day, being followed (not secretly) most days (sometimes twice) and receiving letters, later e-mails my life became hellish—I also received threats to my life.

Thrill seeking and risk taking became my physical need, which I attained through sport. As we've established, I grew up in a competitive equine world, so was no stranger to risk. Running had become a passion and throughout this time it was nothing for me to be knocking out eighty miles a week, in London. This resulted in me travelling the country to run marathons or slightly shorter distances, which wasn't enough to quench my unsettled mind, so weight training accompanied my training. Running didn't allow me to escape though.

Boats were fun too, although river sailing was a little too calm for my preference. Taking them out on adventures on the North Sea was exhausting and dam right freezing but these sea trips were exhilarating. They went some way towards allowing me to forget what was happening within my reality—ironically, that's not something I'm ever going to take for granted again as physically forgetting your past is soul destroying. That said, I do remember having this need to forget—just for a day—what life was like for me and that kinda makes me feel a little guilty. Canoeing was another great escape for me but, again, often a little too calm. This was much more fun after heavy rainfall and after the canals had swollen and the water flow had become rapid.

Climbing seemed like a great adventure too, but our mountains here in the United Kingdom aren't high. My first climb was in Switzerland at 2,970m above sea level. The Schilthorn has the added bonus of a rotating restaurant at the summit where I enjoyed overlooking the valley of Lauterbrunnen in the Bernese Oberland while eating rosti and sausage before embarking on the four-and-a-half-hour hike back to our base. One of three climbs in four days this nine-hour day has happened twice.

I've begun building a picture of how active my life was before taking on the job that changed it. Balancing this side of me with family, study, and voluntary work (as well as my paid job) there was little time to sit down and relax and that meant life was perfect for me. It gave counterbalance to the stress within it. My way of relaxing was to live it to the full.

Doing nothing wasn't on my agenda for that gave me thinking time.

Fascinated by human behaviour, undertaking the role within the premises that housed the person who would completely but temporarily destroy me seemed plausible. Incorporating my therapeutic side, as well as the criminology, there could be no way of knowing after my employment commenced that the restraints would increase in number, due to behaviours getting out of hand. Staff injuries as serious as mine aren't often reported in the news for we sign away our right to speak out and to court action. I'm not one for conformity or silence when things go as wrong as they did for me, especially when matters were avoidable.

Having already elaborated about mirrors, which I believe stemmed from the adrenaline surging through my body after both the bleach attack and the head injury for the same bathroom had been utilised to deal with both incidents. The intent of the first attack was far greater than the injury; the young lady had made a statement to the police that she'd wished she'd shot me, that if she'd been holding a gun, she would have pulled the trigger. While washing blood from my face in the aftermath of the second attack (the head injury) there was a significant time afterwards that was all I saw each time my reflection looked back; the horrific sight from that day; not many months had elapsed between these two events. Topping that, diplopia provided me with two images side by side as my eyesight struggled to work. My eyes refused to focus simultaneously, and each produced an image independently of each other (they still do).

I knew just outside the door there was a change of clothes hanging up, so I'd taken a deep breath, unlocked the door and reached out for it. Nobody was in the staff room, and I ducked back inside. I don't recall how long I stood shivering in the shower or how much blood was lost from my nose. At some point I emerged from the water and had to deal with the bleeding. The hot water wouldn't have helped, I know but my clothes had been soaked through. Dried, changed and now with my damaged clothing bagged appropriately, I ventured out the side door to where the bins were. Nobody noticed my absence—nor cared either what state I might be in or where I was. Adrenaline, at this point, was leaving my body and my hands were beginning to shake uncontrollably. The muscles in my legs were also feeling like jelly. It was at this point the shift manager entered, giving me my next job. I was to be checking they'd administered the correct medication to each patient after the event. Given the attack was during this scenario, I had no idea if the round had been finished, or not, or if anyone else had overseen the medication round. This whole system needs shaking up and I hope what I put my employers through post the attack has opened their eyes to the changes that needed to be made in order to ensure staff safety. The court process also fuelled my adrenaline. It empowered me, which went a long way in giving me some direction when little else had been left.

Despite how much physical and psychological healing my body has achieved, my capability of lifting heavy weights for example and in overcoming PTSD are only fragments of what I was capable of previously. Although I'm efficient at lifting now, my physical strength is nowhere near what it once was. No longer can I hang upside down or bounce about, either. Depth perception is also something of the past—something as simple as catching a ball is a thing of the past. Running would make my brain feel as if it might shatter into a million pieces—and yes there was one summer I tried relentlessly to regain the mile status and it made me monumentally ill. Swimming, although I can force it, causes days of claustrophobia and vertigo and is far from a natural process, yet before my attack I was swimming two miles each week.

Stick me on a boat, however and I'm in my element! For the sake of risk—for arousal—my life changed. I was an addict and didn't know.

Adrenaline seeking has cost me dearly—it almost cost me my life.

Chapter Twenty-Seven

Dealing with Fear

Our 'ego' is fragile and prone to fear but is a structure created of mind, and of learned neural patterns. Sigmond Freud referred to it as the 'id' (impulse life) while societal structure is on the other side. Our ego is designed to interface between impulse life and society—to protect society from impulse life. In order to be afraid, you require self-concept and thus an organism that is functioning instinctively, such as an infant, in each new change in the homeostasis is just a new moment to which it responds. Therefore, it is very delicate to interpret ego and fear due to perception from the position in which we're sitting and the structures around it.

Sensing the way ego works, you are able to see on one hand the extremely powerful impulses in that you might be afraid of, and on the other the tremendous forces outside that you might be afraid of. You can then begin to feel like a very fragile entity within the whole structure. The root of fear is the feeling of separateness that can exist within oneself—that is where fear starts. Once that feeling of separation exists then you process everything from either inside or outside in terms of that model. Your ego then reinforces the feeling of vulnerability due to there being incredibly powerful forces moving both inside and outside of you.

In order to heal there was a need for me to reach inside—deep within—for a spiritual awakening, which I achieved through mediation. Through spiritual work I was able to go behind this model of separation that made me so fragile in order to set me free from being so damaged.

There is still a lot of work to do but I am no longer afraid of my past, instead I embrace it and learn from it—I can talk about it and educate as a result of it. Despite what I might have endured it has strengthened me as a person because I'm not socially ashamed and it no longer hurts me on a social level. I'd be able to stand on a stage and talk about any subject inside this book with confidence and not break down—yet I still feel the need for therapy. This is my ability to separate myself from my reality and know I'm doing so and to realise this isn't a healthy way in healing long-term.

Fear often feeds upon itself and when you're afraid of the fear it gives its greater power—we are afraid because we feel vulnerable. In fairness fear is powerful and once you have conquered how to turn its power into a positive force then wow, what an emotion to embrace! You begin this by letting go of your limiting beliefs, which are the stories you tell yourself about who you are and how your environment affects you and how certain events have impacted you. This is a self-sabotaging cycle we justify by negative thinking, 'if this didn't happen, then this would have.' Instead, even if your story is true, and such events did happen, how they are allowed to affect your life is up to you. Turning fear into power means recognising the source of your fear and to reclaim your life—in order to live your best life!

In doing so you re-write your story. Instead of remaining in the past, dwelling on the negativity you need to acknowledge that your past forms a part of who you are (you cannot change that) and work out a way to discover how it has made you stronger. Perhaps write a list (for now there is only one item on that list, but you can build upon it) as to how that negative event has had a positive outcome.

Self-reflection and positive self-talk are important disciplines that can diminish nervousness, anxiety, and feelings of being afraid and uncertain. Digging deep within yourself often uncovers what's truly going on inside and more often than not self-doubt, that you're not worthy of happiness or success is responsible for fear. These notions are not true, of course but this train of negative thinking is all too easy. Being honest with yourself and identifying the root cause of your fear is the first step in overcoming it—by writing a statement that's empowering but the complete opposite of that negative statement (the opposite of your self-limiting belief) will give you affirmation. Say your powerful statement aloud at the beginning of each day and it will help you strive.

For me, at the time of my most vulnerable state, I used a Marilyn Monroe quote. This was at a time my memory was still unstable and my life in turmoil, "A wise girl knows her limits, a smart girl knows she has none." This quote was the first and last thing I saw each day and is still on display in our home today. Reading it each morning prompted me to push my boundaries further than the previous day, without fear of failing. If I didn't achieve my goal today, there was tomorrow.

Such prompts work better if they're more personal and if spoken aloud, repeated ten times in front of a mirror before your day commences. Yes, that sounds cheesy, but I promise you it's something that's proven to work. You are the only person who has to know that you're speaking to your reflection in the mirror—we've established that wouldn't be something that would have worked too well for me, but the rest of the process had a massive, positive impact.

Making a pros and con's list is another good way of weighing up your options and attaining your passions and visions despite any fears you might have. Trust me when I say there are more pros to acting in the face of fear than the alternative of maintaining a status quo.

Now that your mind is ready, you can act in the face of fear without the whole world crashing down at your feet, which leaves the final step of action.

Taking that first step of actually 'doing' is such a positive feeling of achievement. By far it is the hardest step, of course, and you must remember to take one step at a time. It will get tough so be patient with yourself and allow the process some time. Rewarding your progress will help your mind focus on positive behaviours, so celebrate your successes however small they might be—positive reinforcement really does work and I address this in 'Building a Memory' later in the book.

Choosing to look beneath your surface in order to uncover what's behind your fear allows you to focus on your personal power and become more aligned with who you are and what you might want from life. In turn, pursuing your dreams becomes easier.

There are certain aspects of my life that I feared in the past—violence being one of those things. Given what I've shared with you, I hope I might have your understanding on why that might be the case. Yes, I've been on the receiving end of a lot of it but that doesn't mean I still fear it. Learning self-defence skills in order to protect myself has aided in me overcoming. Partaking in positive steps—including physical activities—in order to better your life allows you to strive. It allows your mind to recover from aspects of your life that would otherwise hold you back.

Empathy

Each face in the crowd tells a story,
Every pair of eyes are windows to a soul.
All the lines and wrinkles you can see,
Are the burdens of someone's goal.

Before you judge why someone might be sad,
Or why they wear a frown upon their face.
Just stop for a moment and ponder,
What brings them to their lonely place.

Can you even begin to contemplate?
What might be on a person's mind?
Would it cost you to show a little empathy?
To a stranger whose world might not be kind?

Chapter Twenty-Eight

Hyper-me

Genetics have meant I'm pre-programmed for a busy life, sitting still has always been, and will continue to be, a difficult task. When faced with the need to relax after my head trauma and because I'd been told I needed to reduce the amount of adrenaline my body produced, or it might just kill me, I had to find alternative ways to entertain myself. What I can only describe as withdrawal occurred. My whole body became vulnerable as my cortisol levels diminished and for the first time in years, I got a cold (which lasted a day). Not only did I miss being active but there was a physical inability to cope with no longer being able to make a choice—I had two needs to stop. Disability was my second.

All of my life had been about action and 'being still' wasn't working for me. Change isn't easy and this was becoming one of the harder aspects I was comprehending. Dealing with stress in the past had meant running eighty miles each week or a spontaneous drive to Cornwall and I couldn't do either of those. Brain trauma physically changed how I would cope—or not.

Action, for a long time could and would only occur on paper. My restless mind vented through poetry (eventually) and moreover in the pages of my thrillers. Although that might not be the same as getting out there and being active it was all I had, and I made that as real as possible. Writing on location for my novels became my goal and priority in order that my emotions became embedded into the storyline as best was possible—if it rained on location, it rained inside my scenes. Many of the storylines and characters are based on my past in some form or another, although each have been twisted into unrecognisable scenarios and quite often the characters are three people rolled into one. If you feel you're along for the ride—that's intentional as I want you submerged, scared, and emotionally committed to the point you forget you've a life of your own.

Although writing tires me psychologically, it doesn't have the same physical effect as sport. Sleep then, doesn't come as naturally as it might and when I've got my mind programmed to write, my mind continues to work throughout the night—it does not rest—it does not know how. There is a notebook with me twenty-four-seven and, yes, I have been known to work right through the night!

Chapter Twenty-Nine

Stormy Nights

Insomnia is one of the most defining symptoms of PTSD. Post brain injury I could sleep for England and was able to do so since childhood. Since however, my sleep patterns have altered. When life is taking a downward spiral towards that dark crack in the earth, I don't sleep at all well, with the slightest of sounds disturbing me. My brain believes it has had a full night's sleep if I'm awoken after ten minutes and that's me awake for the rest of the night. As frustrating as that might sound, I've learnt to switch off the best I can for the alternative is a night of anxious and fretful thoughts disturbing the peace. This works well if the day has proven stress free—but an impossible task if my stress response has been triggered. In such circumstances I'm hyper-vigilant and when the adrenaline passes, tearful as my body struggles to comprehend the chemical changes going on within it once more and I embark on an emotional roller-coaster I cannot control.

There was a time after my head trauma I felt an overwhelming sense that it wasn't safe for me to sleep, which at the time was attributed to the nightmares and flashbacks I was having if sleep did occur (and I addressed this briefly in a previous chapter). It wasn't until nocturnal seizures were diagnosed that it became apparent my life had become more complex than we first thought—that falling asleep was in fact endangering my life. There was a second cycle forming, one of needing sleep to reduce the likelihood of seizures and in being so petrified that one would occur if I did in fact fall asleep. Fear encompassed me as the two storms within my brain battled (again fear of sleep has also been addressed).

I decided that being awake meant the nightmares and flashbacks would be repressed if I could keep my mind active enough. Without sleep, I was under the belief that the nocturnal seizures wouldn't happen—unsurprisingly my reasoning led to exhaustion quickly and my seizures became so uncontrolled they spread to my awake daytime hours too, unfussy if the sun or moon shone.

Needless to say, I knew better than this. My reasoning was unjustified on every level. Being in denial isn't a good place to be however, and it had negative impact on my life, and that of my children. It took a lot of changes to put right again, a lot of effort and research on my part in order to eliminate food triggers for seizures to accompany my medications so they became controlled.

Flashbacks also occurred during daylight hours for my brain was too exhausted to cope. This was all at a time my life was a mess, not long after the brain trauma. By the time I'd realised what I'd done to myself, it took considerable effort in therapy to resolve the hate I felt towards PTSD and years to take control of my life. My PTSD had manifested into scenarios where I'd be so petrified of what was happening inside my mind that I'd retreat into a ball, clothed or naked, and hide myself away. It mattered not if that was during the daytime or at night. Often, I'd come round shaking with fear and cold, finding myself in the empty bathtub, still wet from having bathed or under my kitchen table muddled with the chair legs. Time had lapsed, sometimes hours had passed, and I'd no idea how long I'd lost to fear and my mind taking me back to the time and place of being attacked. The pain I could feel was real inside my head and each time, I'd have to talk myself out of it—knowing that my home wasn't the place I'd been attacked, for that had been at work. This had gone some way towards helping. First, I had to look about to locate myself and often it would take a good thirty minutes for me to realise I was safe within my own environment—I expect it took so long due to the many years of stalking when I wouldn't have felt safe there.

We've discussed fear, and within this chapter I've disclosed a couple of factors I've had to look deep within myself to solve. There is (mainly) no longer fear of having seizures unless I'm suffering with sleep deprivation—after which I do start to be concerned. Infections worry me too, with a combination of the two triggering my seizures with vengeance and a ferocity during the daytime I'd not known before last year it is a worry. Sleep and remaining healthy are, then, important factors to consider. I've also discovered tools to help control my PTSD and through therapy discovered my unconscious mind was more likely to remember the bad stuff than the good.

Repression is designed to protect us but for some reason I've no filter on what might protect me. This is why, in the chapter on 'memory' that follows shortly I speak of where I lock away this type of recall.

Ironically, when there are storms brewing inside my mind and the nights are tough, the only time I get a decent amount of sleep is during a rainstorm or better still, a thunderstorm. There's no point trying to fool my mind with those mood music downloads, however. The storm has to be real and that's got something to do with humidity, the smell of wet soil and everything else that goes with it—my senses pick up on all that goes with mother nature giving it her best.

Epilepsy

There's something dwelling inside my brain,
A storm brewing again and again.
A fog ensuing a confusing stress,
Turning my life upside down into a mess.

It's a fight between epilepsy and me,
I just wish it would leave me be.
When it wins my body stiffens,
I try my hardest, but it won't listen.

Darkness overwhelms as it turns off the lights,
And takes over my body with all its might.
It might tumble me to the floor in a big heap,
At night it makes my body convulse in my sleep.

Memories fade, along with my spark,
A quest of pain, I then embark.
I cannot breathe or hear you speak,
Life suddenly becomes increasingly bleak.

In the past, it's smashed my teeth,

It's torn tendons and my self-belief.

I've bled out and shed many a tear,

As much as I plea, it does not hear.

The monster inside that I fight each day,

for a cure I pray.

Chapter Thirty

Building A Memory

Science has always fascinated me from an early age, and I put that down to a book gifted to me one Christmas by my aunt and uncle around the age of eight—I was certainly extremely young and still at primary school. The theory behind the big bang gripped my imagination. It explained how we evolved as a species—and of how all creatures have changed over millions of years. The subject has fascinated me since then. Charles Darwin became a name that dominated a great deal of my psychological studies over the years as a result. A pioneer of his time he set about changing perception in an age that the correct path would have been to follow the word of Christ and, of course, the creation story. He, however, believed in evolution and I became fascinated in his travel, dedication, and work. Nowadays, I'm the proud owner of antique copies of Darwin's published work—for me owning such old copies of his books gives me goose bumps! That said, I don't dismiss religion although I did as a youngster.

Knowing from an early age my mind was scientific—logical chains of argument making sense of the discourse of the subject through abstract language, my inquisitiveness grew. I'd become a psychotherapist later in life but not before mastering photography professionally—which is considered both an art and also a science. A camera might create art, but it also teaches scientific understanding because you have to measure light, aperture speed and much more in order to capture the perfect image. I've begun relearning the 'art' or 'science' of photography once more and although I'm only using my mobile phone camera, I describe this as learning the science behind bending light once again to create the image I desire. We of course have modern technology these days, with filters that can be added afterwards. Of course, we had that on traditional cameras too—there was always coloured filters that could be fixed onto the end of a camera lens to improve a dull sky but knowing how to use angles and light is much more rewarding.

Knowledge is everything. What we might learn in school is nothing compared to the life lessons or the choices we make. For me learning could (and can never) be quenched and although it had taken a long time to find balance between my busy life and learning goals, I've never stopped filling my brain with new knowledge. Refilling it with forgotten knowledge was, obviously, an unexpected experience and although I've mostly caught up there is still a way to go. For example, there are still many books and films (including classics) I can name but have no idea of the storyline or the names of the characters, yet they line my shelves. Some of the books have been read many times, as indicated by the tell-tale creases along their spines. I lost a lifetime of knowledge and cannot be expected to retrieve that amount in such a short time without putting in a lot of hard graft.

I'm at the point with my recall that I know certain aspects of some memories. For example, I prefer Dickens to Shakespeare but I've no idea why. 'Hard Times' is my favourite Dickens tale—yet I cannot tell you one thing about that book because I've yet to re-read it. This is where I'm at with my life. My pre-injury (and therefore pre-memory loss) life still remains fragmented.

Given the devastating circumstances surrounding my brain trauma and residing complexities of injury I'm thankful memory loss hasn't been permanent. Although I've not returned to the profession of mental health beyond being an advocate of it and speaking on stage about my personal experiences, I do still enjoy the subject matter of psychology and do still read psychology research papers from time to time (most weeks) and am up to date on criminology profiling through published books.

My memory works again. We've established that. However, it functions in a much different way to before (and to how most other people's memories might work). I do of course still have much more to relearn and recall. That aside, I use tools as memory extensions and imagery as a large part of that process. As an extension to my memory palace my family home became a canvas of physical imagery of memorable occasions. Photographs lined my walls in order to prompt those early memories that I made, when my new system was rudimentary—I placed the images in similar positions in the house that I was living inside and also within the memory palace inside my mind in order that I knew where to locate and retrieve it when it was required. It was a process that worked and, over time one that was gradually downscaled as I became more adept at managing the system I'd created.

In order to be creative, my desk becomes an extension to my brain too. That's not as odd as it might first sound! Authors all need a personal space in which to create and each of us do that in our own (often quirky) ways. Surrounding myself with inspiring items that trigger my mind to write is essential for each project. From the books providing research, dictionaries, a candle to trinkets collected while out on adventures (which are inspirational in themselves) are vital to keep my mind flowing. These trinkets could be as simple as a pebble or shell, totally unimportant to anyone else, but for me they have memories embedded into them. A physical reminder of my thoughts, the weather, a conversation, or locations. Most importantly are my note cards and my storyboard that I kept close, as from one session to the next I will not remember my character names or what I've written. Until the first draft of the manuscript is complete, and I read my entire book I won't gain any concept on how much work I have given myself for the various editing stages and it will be during this process that my story will truly come to life. This is the price I pay for having to rebuild my memory. In time, I hope that my determined mindset pays off.

Given quality time to think and process my memory works adequately and I am more than capable at filing what I believe are important things to remember and being able to retrieve that information again at appropriate times. There are situations when it's believed I should have remembered something important to someone else and for me there's no recollection of it ever being mentioned. I'm sure such events will continue to occur in my life and when they do everyone involved just has to move forward and not get cross with me—what's the point? There's nothing I can do to change how things are.

Stress disables this process.

To be stressed, anxious or depressed will mean that my capability of remembering is rendered useless.

Timelines are also a major issue. I might remember an event but there will be no recollection of when or how it may fit into my existence. Even if I know the year and date something occurred, there is not always surrounding events that give any perspective on timing. It's definitely something that needs work as its hugely frustrating to lack the ability and I would imagine this difficult for you to comprehend. Imagine not knowing if you attended a wedding two or six years ago!

Time means nothing other than I know to make the most of it.

Given my degree studies were scientific, that mathematics (particularly statistics) had been such a large part of the research section it might surprise you that, since brain trauma, I can no longer fathom numbers. During my job (in which I was injured), statistics and complex algebra were also important factors—calculating emergency lifesaving medication and medication to sedate patients couldn't go wrong.

Despite the obvious work I still have in bettering my memory, I don't take having one for granted. I've given substantial time to learn how to utilise my new storage system effectively and it is far from the automatic process that most people use. I physically walk the rooms and corridors of my mind in order to store and retrieve my memories. If I choose to read a book you've lovingly written, for example, you will be stored in my internal library visually. Furthermore, sections of your words will be etched into my memory visually too. The quotes I want to remember will be physically written onto a wall I have specifically saved for the purpose. This way, I am going to remember your whole book. This is one of the reasons it takes me a long time to read, if you have photographs in your book all the better—they get placed on another wall. Better still if I'm able to visit the locations inside your book while I'm reading it (and yes, I do that at times). The more imagery I can glean from your work, the more memorable your book is for me. My struggle is real for I also have incredibly poor eyesight too.

Through the process of manually placing memories and being able to wander around the rooms of my mind, I have the ability to visit them at will. Surreal, this process enables me to reflect on my past on my terms, when PTSD isn't a factor affecting my life. This is a far better concept than I'd been facing—the one of not having a future because I couldn't remember anything and had no hope. When PTSD does strike and the door to the cellar (where my bad memories are kept) is left ajar then I'm in huge trouble. All of my traumas seem to escape, and I have no control over what flashback might occur.

I descend into hell.

Every night.

No reprieve.

Deciding to place my sinister memories in a cellar, with the door locked tight came about when I realised the only memories were these awful ones, and it appears there's no filter on me being able to repress these bad happenings of my past. When my new and positive memories begun to mingle among them, I needed the ability to have them separated. Piecing together my past was a long, slow process and affording a designated room for negativity was my way of being able to step outside of the cycle that had been holding me back, so in the cellar they went.

Anyone who has read my first crime trilogy will now relate to why there were so many underground spaces in those books—which was my way of dealing, through writing, with trauma.

Conversations and old photographs shared during reminiscent evenings mean I can share some stories of my childhood with you—fond memories that now live on in my heart that can be shared with future generations.

As you might imagine, my childhood was focussed on our animals and the fun we had with them but there was also a lot of fun with my cousins. With regards to the ponies and horses, there was a distinct bond formed between myself and Snudge, my first pony. He was quite the character and responsible for my courage. My confidence while riding him, compared to the shy child I was when not was remarkable. Once I'd seen the man who would become my hero up close and personal fly through the air, defying gravity on his stunt motorbike, something shifted in me. Those of you who know me personally and who have read *Lost Soul* will know that's Eddie Kidd OBE, and that he jumped the River Blackwater in Maldon, Essex from one side of a demolished viaduct to the other. My grandparents lived along the lane on the landing side of that stunt, and I watched from the field just up from where they lived, aged seven. Eddie is still known as 'The Black Knight' and that jump was for the film 'Flying High.' This was an all-defining moment in my life which enabled me to experience thrills of my own. I believe, looking back, that I have sought adrenaline since. That's not something I regret.

Our equine pals owned phenomenal manners either to ride or in the stable, but rarely both. More often than not they had a spark when ridden that was a whole lot of fun. I'd moved up a size of pony and being bolted with on a regular basis just became part of what I did on Sundays at the age of ten—jumping a mini on one of those days added to the thrill of it all (I'm sure my parents put superglue in my jodhpurs). That was the day

I became the stunt rider I'd aspired to be! I was thrilled, joyous and excited. Unfortunately, my parents hadn't enjoyed this day as much as I and put a stop to these antics. They decided it was time to move up another size and 'Bumble' as he was called had to go. They put me on the safest animal to ride possible, and to be fair I learnt a lot. She was my cousin's pony, 'Fern.' Another went faster backwards than it did forwards so that had to go back—we'd never seen anything quite like it to be honest. 'Fred' came a few down the line, and he was a character. A few sizes up he was a horse with the mindset of a 'bad boy' and was right up my street—if he'd have been human, he'd have come complete with leathers and a Harley.

One day eventing became our challenge and trust me dressage truly was the challenge, as it really was a little on the calm side for my horse and me. Both of us enjoyed the adrenaline rush of the show jumping and cross country a little too much. The funniest comment I ever received during a dressage test was that my horse was "disobedient at X." Translated, this meant that he'd decided to be a rocking horse rearing and bucking on the spot (he refrained from farting, whereas Snudge would have enjoyed a good ol' fart). He'd had refused to stand still while I did the right and proper thing that is etiquette within the discipline—I was saluting the judge and trying my hardest not to giggle. I did of course smirk which he sensed, and of course this encouraged him all the more. Some months down the line I had a group riding lesson from the same judge, and she learnt for herself what a handful 'Fred' was. As one of the calmest ladies I've met I let her have a ride on him and he played up something rotten. I knew he would—the only person he was ever calm for was my mother!

Dad raced. His horse was large at seventeen hands and by the age of fourteen I'd stopped growing. At five foot four I knew I'd lost my battle with height and would be 'vertically challenged' for life. That's not a matter to have held me back. I enjoyed taking her out, something that didn't take much to talk my father into, mother was a different matter though. My argument was that most jockeys were shorter than me and I was as physically strong as anyone my size.

Although I've digressed with regards to age, I felt it best to keep subjects together. A quick rewind back to my earlier years and to a special friend. Humeza forms some of my earliest recollections. From Pakistan, she joined my cousin's family when I was approximately five years old, she was in England for her education. I owe Humeza my ability to lip read for she is deaf. This learnt skill is something I still use today, another way for me to communicate during tough times. Luckily, I do have photographs of us all together and am still in touch with her. We reminisce of our times together and it is my hope to see her again one day, where I dream it will be possible to celebrate the strength of women the world over.

Primary school is nothing but a blur of attempts to be at home, from which I can only remember a select few names of my peers. Three to be precise. One teacher remains in my mind for what he did (but not his name). Unsure of how his learning techniques would fare in today's world, personally I cannot thank this man enough for the foundations that were laid down in my mind at the time. Not only did he give me the confidence to further my education then but now, post injury, I know there is the ability to build a better logic-base for myself. Logic can be taught; it doesn't have to come naturally. Through his reward system—

of galaxy chocolate—we, as a class, were taught gradually more difficult logic intelligent quotient puzzles. Those that worked them out fastest were rewarded with chocolate. Not only were we learning to be intelligent but to strive in a competitive world too. I've had four children go through primary and secondary school and three of them (so far) through university with my fourth there now. Not once have they mentioned teaching quite like this! For me it was the beginning of how positive reinforcement worked which would be covered at much more depth during my psychological studies and also in my place of work where I was brutally attacked.

During my thirties I was being pressured from several angles. Not all angles were positive, but some were. One of those pressures was to apply to MENSA and I'm so glad I relented as becoming registered helped me gain help after my head injury. Having a registered Intelligence quotient (IQ) to compare with what was a considerable drop in ability finally showed how much brain damage with which I was living. My cognitive [in]ability—reasoning, logic, and problem-solving—was gone. Thanks to the primary teacher, whose name I wish I could recall, I know my brain can be retrained and that my capability will return and I know this because I have made considerable progress already and through my studies know there are countless psychological trials giving reward to the subject when they perform the desired action in order—they associate the action with the reward and thus they do it more often. The reward becomes the reinforcing stimulus—positive reinforcement works.

I am not a pigeon (sorry that's a psychology joke)!

Despite it not being great for the waistline: note to self—add chocolate to the shopping list!

After the transition to secondary school, there was a definite focus of sport in my life. I'd started running at an early age and at my first senior school was lucky enough to have some tuition by Olympian, Daily Thompson who is famed for his Olympic gold medals in nineteen-eighty and eighty-four in the Decathlon. I am proud of this, and it stood me well later in life when I'd start competing in tetrathlon. Never a sprinter, it was evident from eleven I'd be a distance runner and having an affinity to run straight through the middle of the mud—or a stream—without hesitation, cross country would be up there with my favourite disciplines. To this day I will jump in a puddle rather than walk around it (and have been known to do so in heels). I'm not one of those squealy-girl types and to be fair this placed me ahead of my gender at such a young age.

Moving at the age of twelve to where my parents still live saw a change of schools. You either fitted in or didn't where we moved to back then, a location much more rural to what I was used to. Being shy and small it was assumed I'd be physically weak, but they were very much mistaken. Quietly feisty would have been a better description. I've a hidden strength that comes from years of sport and stacking hay and straw bales. Despite being tiny I could arm wrestle anyone willing to take me on—and they took me on thinking they'd win my dinner money.

They didn't take me on twice!

Stacking hay brings me to wonderful summer memories. According to one of my cousins, I was doing a day's work on their family farm by the age of six. Alongside the adults during haymaking season us kids would be on the trailer hand stacking bales of hay all weekend long and by the time we reached nine each of us were doing our fair share of pitch forking them onto the trailer too. Haymaking season with my aunt and uncle had advantages and often ended up with a plate of pancakes or a cake, which are two different stories I could also share.

Other farm stories have us cousins cringing now we are adults and others leave unanswered questions. We would be sent into the horse field with a basket to collect mushrooms—we distinctly remember them growing in fairy circles and having the instruction that if we could peel them, they would be edible. Knowing what we know now, that if we got it wrong, it could have been deadly, we don't actually know if we ate them or if they were thrown away and we were sent out to collect them just for the fresh air. We ate them! We all knew what field mushrooms looked like but not sure that, at our age, knew they needed to have brown or tan gills. My aunt would have known that the ones with white gills would have poisoned us, maybe she wouldn't have, who knows?

Skating on the duck pond was always great fun once it had frozen over. Looking back now, none of us know how deep it was. I'm not exactly tall as an adult and as a child was a squirt of a thing! Given you can drown in an inch of water and if the ice had of cracked, one of us might have gone through. We now know just how crazy it was that we did this, especially as we were unsupervised.

These days health and safety are extremely strict with regards to children on farms and for good reason. Luckily, we didn't hurt ourselves other than the usual grazed knee or scratch. Haystacks are a particular attraction, and let's face it kids do love dens. Ours were spectacular with corridors and rooms reinforced with wooden rafters for a roof so the structure didn't collapse. Given the nails protruding from the wooden reinforcements, how we didn't gash open our heads, or hands when jamming them into place, or manoeuvring under them, we'll never know.

Survive we did, and all the better for the freedom of our era. The fresh air and imagination that our generation survived on, compared to the computer and gaming generation of today was our blessing.

Having studied criminology and psychology, of being exposed to research papers detailing the effect of gaming on young minds, and the detrimental long-term damage that killing within games does—that bludgeoning or shooting inside a game and a young mind watching that 'dead' person just getting back up can, sometimes, give an impressionable mind the wrong image of reality—I know what kind of upbringing I'd rather.

My cousin's and I had fun, whatever the location. At the boundary hedge, right at the bottom of the lower field, there was space for another den. For us this gave us the space for stinging nettle battles—our 'sword' fights took place here, nettles or sticks. Our battle bruises the welts from being stung or a gentle jab from a stick. Nothing sinister—just kids messing about. Wild roses grew in the hedge and once the hips formed, they provided itching powder. This was as un-innocent as we became!

These days innocent battle weapons are replaced with knives and the innocent turns into warfare between youths on the streets that result in unwarranted deaths. The freedom of our time is a rare phenomenon these days for even in the countryside the crimes of urban life has caught up in our quiet areas, albeit not to the same level or frequency.

Only two of us cousins were female, and we often went and stayed at our grandparent's together (which is the house that forms my memory palace now). Sharing a double bed with my older cousin meant we could chit chat late, but it was also inevitable there'd be a little mischief along the way. More often than not, as the youngest, I'd be on the receiving end and without warning the colouring or other activity we might be doing would stop and I'd suddenly be immobilised so that the tickling would commence. Back then the slightest tickle would have me in fits of giggles and my cousin would have me laughing until I burst—literally. As our grandmother rushed through the bedroom door declaring us "naughty girls" (and I can hear her voice as I type this) we'd both be in fits of giggles together. I was seriously young back then and today, not one part of me is ticklish for my cousin expelled any 'tickly' that might have remained out of me!

Chocolate was a huge treat growing up and certain aspects of those chocolaty traditions from back then remain in my life now. Christmas was a time of family 'get togethers' and the Quality Street tin would emerge. Remaining loyal to this, my children and I have created our own tradition and as the tree goes up, out come the Quality Streets as a mark of the beginning of our own Christmas celebrations. Chocolate isn't so much a treat now as it was back in the seventies, so saving this particular confectionery for this time of year is special for us. For me, tradition helps me remember too. Through these acts, I'm able to reflect and remember my past—repeating behaviours has been an important part of remembering.

This brings me to return visits to locations my children and I visited on holidays together. Much of their lives are still missing from my memory, which although heart breaking, has started to correct itself. Through re-joining English Heritage, which was a large part of our lives, and returning to places the children and I had been in the past, not only triggers memories of that place to return but ones of the surrounding areas and of that time came flooding back too.

Once memories begin to return there is a knock-on effect and several appear simultaneously. There is then a struggle to comprehend the amount of information that's forthcoming. An overwhelming quantity of data that needs manually placing inside my memory palace alongside the ordinary day-to-day stuff becomes overpowering. Inevitably, something will get forgotten and you can bet that will be an appointment that shouldn't be.

Fourteen was the age at which I found a sudden confidence. Partly due to my cousin, Emma being around more and very much due to the fact we both joined a club. Since this time, we've built a repertoire of stories and many evenings have been spent sat around our tables, where I've shared 'Emma and I' stories. These won't be shared here as they are personal to her as much as they are to me—they are not just mine to blurt out. One day we may sit down and write them out together but given what we used to get up to between us, please don't hold your breath! Our children love being a part of our secrets that we've shared with them—family stories passed down to the next generation and laughter shared. My lot know if it begins 'Emma and I...' they are in for a treat and that I've remembered something new. They also think they've led a tame life in comparison and could have pushed the boundaries a little harder with me!

Anyhow, through this club we did some serious partying but also some wonderful learning. The basis of my public speaking was formed here, albeit in debating—I could reword it was where learning to argue professionally commenced (and that's not something you want to get into with me). Although out of depth against the adults at fourteen, this wasn't the case inside school, and I'd suddenly found a voice in the classroom. Debating was part of our English lessons, and I was beginning to be noticed. My other English work improved at this time too, and when pulled aside by my teacher and told that a career in writing should be considered, it was met with laughter. Yet here I am, several decades later with several books under my belt within a short timeframe! She saw a gift all those years ago within my scientific mind that was eager to emerge.

Since the age of fifteen, I've had a passion for photography. Also discovered through this same club, which provided opportunities to enter my images into competitions—one per year—that won in their category. At thirty-two I became a professional wedding and corporate photographer and had my own business covering Kent that ventured, commercially into London. I've also been known to throw the camera around my neck and jump onto a rib (speed boat) to capture sailing boats race, which was the most thrilling experience of what I did.

Falling in love with cars happened at this club too. Yes, I am a petrol head. Learning to drive (on private land) at fourteen was a privilege—as was driving the beautiful cars I was let loose in. One of the funniest driving memories I'm willing to share is that my school locker key from sixth form fitted a friend's Ford Escort. Sneaking out into the car park (okay so that wasn't very private) I would move his car and enjoy the baffled look on his face as he walked to where he was [rightly] convinced he'd parked, while I waited for my school bus. He was a year older than me, so I only got away with this for a few months until he left. Confessing after his last A-level exams was priceless.

I've driven some of the most amazing cars under the most incredible circumstances in my time: that need for speed having been embedded within me from so young. Driving is the one thing I miss terribly as a direct result of having been assaulted. For me this is more than a lack of independence. Returning my driving licence meant I'd miss out on the experience and the thrill of being in control of acceleration, of handling corners—braking just at the right moment in order that momentum isn't lost. Being a passenger isn't the same, you cannot feel the horsepower through the steering wheel like you can when you're handling a beautiful performance car. As with everything I do, I didn't just pass my test and drive for the rest of my life—I'd experienced skid pans, racetracks, and off-roading. I'd driven tracked vehicles, performance cars, minibuses, and even combine harvesters. I never got around to taking my HGV or motorbike tests and I should have. In hindsight, you never know what's around the corner and you should always make the most of all opportunities. For me, not driving has left a black hole equivalent to the one I've already spoken about.

Physics is beautiful. Its powerful. Its art—driving is a science.

Chapter Thirty-One

Returning to Hell

Falling back into hell for a second time came as a shock, initially. Although I knew the possibility was there, never had there been any indication it would have been anything but returning to the room in which I was beaten and in which I received my head trauma. Despite being able to talk about this incident, there are aspects of it I'm prohibited to discuss unless in a professional setting and thus there are times I could benefit from a conversation when I must be silent. This can cause tension and conflict within my mind as you might imagine.

Never had I imagined I'd ever return to the turmoil of when I nearly lost my youngest daughter and the events that controlled my life afterwards. Understandably, this was an extended period of time (nine years in total) to have been exposed to repeated traumatic experiences before calmness returned to my life and a further period of time before I was able to stop looking over my shoulder expecting my stalker to be following me.

My point is that, although I knew there was no risk from the people who caused such turmoil in my life and from the fact that I'd forgiven these acts of cruelty in order for me to move forward in my life they affected my unconsciousness.

PTSD cannot be underestimated.

Emotions, for me, are a key factor to gauge how I'm doing and what's going on deep inside of me. The poem that follows, 'Depression' is how I begin feeling when things are not sitting right within my psyche.

At this point in my life anxiety isn't a factor as it's been eliminated due to the medication that I've sought myself. I know if it weren't for this that its likely PTSD would be a huge worry for me again. Constant demands placed upon me from outside sources are high, but I'm determined they won't break me again for I'm not prepared to revisit times in my life during which I feared for it any longer—as it's an unsettling concept.

My second encounter with PTSD involved someone that once nurtured me, which made it all the worse. Having to conquer fear is exhausting to the point of breaking when faced with life/death scenarios on a daily basis (and that was my reality for a long time). My reality now is to stop my body releasing stress hormones in order that I can commence pain relief and start to feel myself again.

Many other daily 'normal' life occurrences also trigger stress responses within me, and some might surprise you. I spent time in my second therapy sessions coming to terms with the smell of coffee. It was on the breath of my rapist and also the man who assaulted me at work, who disabled me. I can now walk into a coffee shop but having the stuff breathed over me is another matter. Exposure therapy has its boundaries! Alarms sounding, shouting and the smell of stale urine or it not flushed away can also trigger me. The kitchen is a major trigger and I've dedicated a chapter to why.

Through therapy it became possible to sit and write in a coffee shop, which I achieved weekly. The tools I learnt enabled me to cope with alarms, but nothing can ever change how stale urine will make me feel nor how being shouted at or to have 'coffee breath' on me will make me crash as both make me die a little inside.

My PTSD triggers don't send me into instant flashback where I'd spend half the day under the dining room table or naked in the bath—for which I'm thankful. If they catch me by surprise and do occur, they lower me down a rung or two on the ladder towards the crack in the earth that swallows me whole. I'm forever fighting to remain 'un-depressed' (if I can dare use that as a term) diligently attempting to keep my head above the water.

Due to a combination of medications that have side effects of depression and three anaemias (two of which have side effects of depression) I suffer low mood often. That said, I've never felt suicidal. Survival shouldn't carry such severe consequences as extreme depression but, unfortunately it does. My symptoms are recurrent, which means they vanish and then return. During episodes that depression is with me there's always a feeling of isolation—a disconnection if you like—from those around me. I feel unwanted and not appreciated that's accompanied by a sense of abandonment. I'm not unwarranted in feeling this way as I can go hours without speaking or seeing anyone despite being in the same household at times and more often than not this is when I'm feeling at my most vulnerable this occurs.

In understanding my last comment, I'd like to highlight where these feelings stem from—for I've spent considerable time analysing myself during my healing process and while authoring this book: after being raped I disconnected myself from the possibility of ever being in a trusting relationship with a man. I did, of course attempt a couple that failed. Through therapy I learnt to trust men again (at a distance), but I most definitely had walls of defence in place. Over the years I've become self-reliant because that way my heart couldn't be hurt.

Until now.

Those walls of defence came crashing down, I opened up, gave my whole self and now at my utmost time of need, when my depression is at its worse, I'm often on my own. I have already shared why I feel this way in my chapter on 'Loneliness' and touch on this further in the chapter 'Dissociation and Reliving' that's coming up.

Looking back at my trauma experiences it is easy to detect a pattern. As a ten-year-old seeking help and having my mouth washed out with soap (by a man); at thirty I was raped (by a man); between two-thousand-and-six and twenty-twelve I was stalked (by a man); at forty-two I was assaulted that caused disability (by a man).

Depression

Shush, listen. Can you hear my screams?
So silent, they echo inside my dreams.
No? For my emotion hides behind a smile,
Beneath a dark path I travel, mile upon mile.

Silent screams always falling upon deaf ears,
Continuing to haunt me all these years.
Drowning in silence, I'm really not fine,
Screams of depression swallowing my mind.

Happiness trickling through my fingers,
Being replaced with darkness that lingers.
Like attempting to hold water in your hands,
Grasping it impossible, as it disappears into the sand.

Attempting to climb back through the crack in the earth,
Doubting every aspect of my self-worth.
Suffocating as I withdraw down into the abyss,
Towards the black mist that's given me its death kiss.

Chapter Thirty-Two

Dissociation and Reliving

Overwhelming trauma can become split off and fragmented. This means the emotions, sounds, images, thoughts, and physical sensations related to the traumatic event take on a life of their own with parts—or fragments—of the memory intruding upon the present. Trauma is quite literally relived until the memory of it is resolved.

Stress hormones secreted by the body that are designed to protect you in flight-fight-freeze situations continue circulating and your defensive movements and responses replay. Once this negative cycle commences it can be triggered by the smallest irritation that's unrelated to the original trauma. The person suffering may not realise the significance as to why such a minor matter is making them believe they are about to be annihilated. What they are unaware of is the chemical warfare occurring inside their body that we've already discussed at length.

If the initial trauma wasn't bad enough, flashbacks and reliving are in many ways worse. As strange as that might seem trauma does have a beginning, a middle and an ending—at some point it will be over and there is always a point that the victim (or better put the survivor) can say 'I felt safe when….' There are always circumstances where this is not the case and trauma that is continuing, such as war zones and those suffering from domestic abuse are two examples.

For those who go on to endure the symptoms of PTSD, a flashback can occur at any time. They can be awake or asleep and there is no way of predicting when they might happen, or indeed for how long each episode might last. Unsurprisingly, for those of us who have known environmental triggers we go about our lives arranging life with military precision in order to protect ourselves, as far as humanly possible, against flashbacks occurring (especially in public). This is known as avoidance.

On a personal note, I avoid alarms sounding as they will trigger me to suddenly be transported into the room in which I was attacked. One of two things happen once I'm there—either I'm able to control what happens next through grounding techniques or I go through the whole process of being assaulted. If the latter happens my flashback lasts the duration of the attack, I feel the physical sensation of every punch, each emotion and hear every sound and smell, each foul stench of the place.

Its horrific—my mind gives me two seconds to act and if I'm not feeling on top of the world, if I'm stressed for example, or if I've been exposed to an alarm sounding for an extended time period this struggle becomes more difficult.

Replaying traumatic events combined with the release of stress hormones engrave these memories deeper into the mind. Our ordinary daily events become less compelling as a result. What is happening around us, the normal day-to-day aspects of our life, becomes boring which makes the things that used to bring us joy more difficult to concentrate on. As we become more distant from 'normal' life we no longer associate ourselves as belonging in the present. Concentrating on living in the here and now takes much more effort and, thus our mind fixates on living in the past—meaning our trauma has imprisoned us.

Triggered responses (such as an alarm sounding being one of mine) are personal to each of us. These reactions might seem irrational, but they are outside our control. They make PTSD sufferers feel numb, often to the point there might not be an emotional response at a family funeral or at a celebration party. In turn this can bring on a powerful feeling of shame, which is the dominant emotion of PTSD—it results in hiding the truth, something we become preoccupied in.

Relearning how to feel is an important part of the therapeutic process which begins by having empathy for yourself. This may well be the hardest hurdle to overcome but it goes a long way towards your healing. Through trauma our brain function has changed. Our threat-perception system to physical danger and also to other people's reactions is now dictated by the imprint of our past and what began as an outside inference, is now played out by an internal battle inside our bodies. What we need is mastery over the trauma, the sensations, and emotions—this begins with how we feel and empathise about ourselves.

Without any doubt I've made no secret that I hit rock bottom after being assaulted. You only have to trawl through my Instagram posts or read *Lost Soul*, and that information is freely shared. Pressing the self-destruct button wasn't a choice, the road to self-oblivion wasn't a journey taken through chance. When choice is removed, and you are left facing unexpected decisions it is all-to-easy to give up.

Don't get me wrong, I'm not sat here typing and feeling sorry for myself. I'm far from a quitter and, frankly, had I not lived the life I've led do not believe I'd be where I am today. Facing death changes you, and it changes your perception on the world. It's your choice if you decide to make your life better than it was before, or not. However, for that to happen there has been a great deal to accept before moving forward in life.

During the assault, I disassociated (had an outer body experience). This was the beginning of me not remembering and over the next few days as after-shock events occurred, my memory evaporated as if someone was pouring them out from a water jug—this is the second analogy I've used (the first being doors closing). Ironically, it's a sensation I now recall—the harder I attempted to retain my memories the faster they became out of reach, leaving an emptiness behind them. Distant from all I'd known, and desperate to get my life back I was left frustrated, frightened, and angry. No longer recognising myself or anyone around me, I have some insight of what it's like to be old with dementia. My grandmother had Alzheimer's disease and I wish I'd understood this more back when I was a teenager and in my early twenties, for I could have made her life more comfortable.

Coming home from hospital a cowering wreck, I hid in the shadows of my existence and floated above myself, continuing to experience a disconnected life the majority of the time. I'd lost the ability to understand my internal world and the ability to cope in an external one, but I'd learnt how to dissociate. There was a long road ahead of me as, through listening to the interactions of my children (whose names I'd relearnt in hospital) I gradually learnt to cope. Through them, I learnt how to live and to strive. As a family we adapted. Expectations of me as a mother changed and that role has been difficult to take back. Instead, I've had to settle to equal standing in our relationships, despite being the one who continued to pay the bills—a small price to pay, when your children have stepped up and taken responsibility for you at such young ages. My youngest was eleven when she became my carer and only twelve when she won a Jack Petchy Foundation Award for doing so.

Promoting therapy—because despite what I've shared I do believe in therapy—has become one of the subjects I advocate. There was a time however, that my faith in that process waivered. Reliving the assault in the first round of therapy had catastrophic and long-lasting complications for me and this process was blamed for the seizures I was having. A prominent psychiatrist (who was independent to my personal medical team) diagnosed that due to this process in combination to a court case could induce psychological seizures. Somehow my neurologist got handed this document and dismissed me from her books.

Yes, those therapy sessions were vividly traumatic but in a controlled environment. They gave me an opportunity to face the event, exposing me to every aspect of the attack that caused me distress. And although I wasn't ready to face it back then, it allows me to cope better now. Those sessions were far from pretty and they revealed the severity of the attack.

Despite not having a diagnosis of epilepsy, the fact that medication controls my seizures tells me and my doctors that my seizures are not psychological. Also, during extreme stress and periods of PTSD more recently, I didn't have a single seizure. The only time they return is during times of bacterial infection—such as kidney infections. My pain levels sit at an eight/ten most days and my seizures are still under control thanks to the medications I've been prescribed. My fight to get a diagnosis will continue, simply for peace of mind.

I've digressed, for which there's no apology. My first re-living experience showed that I may as well have entered the boxing ring without training and now way of fighting back—my opponent, being obsessed with Mohammed Ali had studied the form of his hero for years and he could pack a punch. Add to that the strength of a man in psychosis and you begin to get the feel of what I was facing alone.

Isolated.

Depersonalised.

Scared.

In hell.

This might give your further insight into why I feel so isolated and abandoned as described in the previous chapter.

Coping with outer body experiences is simple, you have to ground yourself. If my first therapist did something correct, she certainly taught me how to refocus and stop this from happening. We went through the necessary grounding protocol at the beginning of each session and from this I knew my buttocks were firmly placed in my seat with my bare feet firmly on the carpeted floor. With the window open, I could hear birds singing, and feel the cold air hitting my face. That I had survived and was here, alive, and in this room with her, completed the 'here and now' facts I was to remember.

There was only an intention to return to the 'attack room' for a few seconds that first time but like all my memories that return this one gushed back with such ferociousness she kept it going. Tears streaked my face and my body heaved through the experience. She witnessed my outer body experience just as I'd done so originally and wanted me to stop but I kept it going.

Intense was an understatement.

By the time I was finished, my whole body trembled with fear, as adrenaline rushed through my veins. Information that had been fragmented suddenly hit my senses and the sensations that had been suppressed for months were suffocating me. Allegedly, I'd been quite animated throughout, but now exhaustion was taking over.

I'd got some answers though and this woman hadn't written anything down except a few random words—she wasn't going to be called as a witness in my court case because what went on in her room was private between her and her client and I appreciated that. She would have to make a statement at some point however, but they wouldn't make sense of her notes if they asked for them.

Gradually, over the weeks every minute second was added, which is where the sounds and smells of the trauma materialised. I'm not sure I needed this much information in all honesty. For too long there were too many triggers for nightmares and flashbacks, and although this trauma was no longer fragmented those flashbacks did still occur. Running water was a major factor at the time and I still don't like water on my face to this day.

What should have been helping resolve my PTSD appeared to be making it worse and despite my symptoms becoming heightened, I was discharged from therapy. Disillusioned, it wasn't until I met a consultant at St Thomas' in London (the independent psychiatrist) who convinced me I should try again. The good doc gave me a long list on why and how therapy would and could help all these months down the line and convinced me to embrace the notion. I did however refuse to see the same therapist, for I needed someone older than myself. This person would be the first man I would come to trust outside of immediate family, and it was him who taught me that it was okay to place trust in others, particularly in men. I've spoken of him previously—Gary (the not going swimming with you guy).

In order to heal I've had to get extremely uncomfortable, for my past hasn't been a ride in the park, as you've now learnt.

Chapter Thirty-Three

Cycle of Doom

Having spent so many years being downtrodden, which continued and intensified while I was being stalked, I wanted to know why people changed. Additionally, there was personal necessity to know why others had the need to control and, ultimately, why victims allowed it to happen. Setting out on a new path of discovery, I commenced studying. Becoming a qualified psychotherapist was the first step in this process. It set out a foundation upon which to base the rest of my learning upon. Studying criminology and psychology was the next step, which would occur as home study. Determined to take this all the way to a PhD, my aspirations were high—of course my courses would have taken me to university on campus eventually.

In understanding how the mind might go wrong as an adult, it is first vitally important to understand child development and what might go wrong in those early years. The subject areas I studied were harsh—at times they were cruel—at whatever the age the subjects might have been. Ultimately, I found it more difficult to deal with the circumstances of when children murder children. As time progressed, I naturally fell into a specialist area. That too wasn't a pleasant one to be in but there was vested interest. Ironically, as part of my course I studied brain injury (specifically sport related). It is then an area of expertise I'm familiar with.

Taking on a role that utilised my knowledge, therapeutically as well as from a criminology point of view, felt like the right decision to make. I'd escaped my stalker—who had only relented three months previous—and I was stepping straight into another danger zone. Looking back reflectively on my behaviour now, and at what I have been through in the past, this was only going to end in disaster. I should have known better—I should have stepped away.

In fairness it should have been thirteen years earlier that this action should have occurred, when there were plans to have moved away from the area in which we lived. What a simple solution this would have been, but I was stopped. Those thirteen years have, without doubt, had a huge impact on my life and now, living with PTSD it is me that lives with the consequences. I hold myself responsible for my actions—or better phrased in-action and thus own that my mental health has taken a downward turn.

Instead, I endured and later entered this new phase of working life. A life in which I'd be exposed to danger on a daily basis. This was, of course, part and parcel of what I was expected to deal with for we were all trained to de-escalate or if the behaviour got out of hand, restrain. Needless to say, restraint was used more often than not. Adrenaline pumped through my veins more often than it didn't—I no longer required those long runs amounting to eighty miles per week or my other sporting adventures.

I just turned up at work!

After the several instances I've mentioned elsewhere in the book, I was left fighting to regain myself. I'd lost everything after the brutal attack that left me with brain damage.

For those of you who have read *Lost Soul* and know I cannot remember all of my children's childhood memories, some of what I has been shared, might now give you an insight into why that might be. In particular, it is my youngest that was affected the longest by this, yet our bond couldn't be stronger. As time passes and my eldest has given me a grandchild, this has prompted some of those memories to return. Time is indeed a great healer and memories do return when prompted by other events.

This gives me hope for the future.

Stepping away from the cycle of doom was a conscious decision. One I made in order to heal back in twenty-eighteen and one I'm having to make again now. It takes strength and courage to stand up tall and say, "no more" and to mean it. It certainly takes stamina to sustain that decision. Life changes are made easier with the support of one's family and I'm privileged that my children all champion me in all I do. Part of this process, for me, was to step away from the area I'd lived in for so long. This had been my intention for many years. Had I not met Dave I'd not be fifty miles away but two-hundred miles away in Yorkshire or further afield still. In order to do this, I sold our family home—the one in which I bought my children up as a single parent.

Speaking out via books and on social media has been difficult at times but also hugely rewarding. Such decisions were mind-blowing and daunting in the beginning but now form part of my identity. I keep my children separate from my public life, they don't comment on my social media posts and their photographs are hidden from view on my profiles. This might seem extreme but that's the way we like it. Their privacy is vitally important to me.

Stepping outside of the cycle that creates negativity is all-important as until you've done so you cannot recognise damaging and dangerous behaviours aimed towards you. I've studied human behaviour on scales that would shock most, both academically and also within the workplace. Watching these behaviours unfolding in people that you know is enlightening. When these people no longer have the ability to reach you then that feeling is wholesome. It means you've risen above their games, that you are no longer consumed by them—owning your headspace means you don't give them room within it.

Chapter Thirty-Four

Remembering in Order to Heal

During my healing process I'd Often came around to the words, "I do worry about you." Usually, we were in the car, and I'd gone quiet and that's definitely something my partner isn't used to. Under normal circumstances there'd always be a great deal to be discussing—our plans for the day ahead, a project we have on the go or simply the banter between us. Our conversations are varied and often comical. At times of crisis, I'm captured in a deep and desperate state which takes every ounce of reserve remaining in continuing to be composed. Conversation of any kind with me in this state would reduce me to tears, for I'm done—I'm at the point of exhaustion. Surviving back in April twenty-fourteen would be a waste of energy if my life had of been reduced to a constant state of this, so my fight had to be stronger and this time around, it had been so personal.

All too often the content of my mind is dark as I self-reflect on my past, which is (unfortunately) part of my way forward. Effectively, when I go quiet and seem withdrawn, more often than not, it isn't always negative thinking. It is, instead, because I'm working deep within myself on my most complex issues and looking for that way forward. Given that my latest therapy was withheld I've not had a choice in this and thus a cross I've had to endure alone. The other half, as lovely as he is, isn't equipped or qualified as a therapist, and so this is a journey I've embarked upon myself. There wasn't often 'alone time' when it was required so car journeys seemed the time for me to undertake this task.

The important and most relevant traumas in my life are burdens not easily shared and they most certainly didn't fall within the realms of normality. To be refused professional help to get through them threw me a curve and as a result it took longer to recover than it should. Ploughing through this complicated time has meant research and hours of reading but resulting from my dedicated attitude to healing I've the satisfaction of knowing that I've a strength within me to cope under immense pressure. I've also relearnt the ability to say "no" when its most needed in order that I remain healthy of mind—for without that I am nothing.

Rediscovering research has been enlightening and rewarding too. Furthermore, I've rekindled my scientific side that I'd loved before brain injury. In a sense that's been as healing as the therapeutic side of relearning meditation and coping tools. Learning and progressing most definitely won't be stopping here, for, as this book ends, the next will commence.

As with any recovery journey this is one that I will always be travelling. For as long as there are memories to recall I believe PTSD will be the way in which I will begin the remembering process. That doesn't mean each episode is negative as some of my flashbacks are actually positive ones, fragmented still, but gradually over time my life is piecing together. I instinctively know when a nightmare is a memory returning or an irrelevant dream—certainly flashbacks during my awake times are experiences repeating themselves (remembered or returning memories).

The quiet, silent moments are lessening as time passes and I begin to feel less suffocated by life and all it encompasses. Depression, when it arrives, hinders this. Some of the chemical reactions remain, which is the next phase for me as limiting this will also reduce the constant pain that I suffer—as the stress response lessens, the inflammation will begin to subside.

There is misconception that victims of PTSD or better put, survivors of trauma, should let go of their past and live for today or their future. That they shouldn't dwell, instead embrace change, and move on. For the record, I love change—I live for change. As for letting go of my past, I wish it would let go of me. I'd love nothing more. Letting go, however, would eliminate the possibility of a future.

Instead embracing the past and accepting it has formed who I've become and owning my story is the way forward.

Chapter Thirty-Five

Living Free

Feelings of relief and freedom, once the symptoms of PTSD subside and a sense of control returns, is like having the weight of the world removed from my shoulders. There is, of course, the knowledge that the symptoms will always remain a part of me—that they'll never vanish completely. Believing I'll be symptom free would be to bury my head in the sand, and to live a lie. PTSD forms part of my identity and thus I embrace it.

Freedom, then, is to be in control of my thoughts and how I deal with the trauma I've experienced. In deciding when and if I think about my past and having the ability to discuss it places me in a great position to live out the future. Therapy, now it has been guaranteed since moving to another area of the country, will enable me to do this faster. In between times, knowing that I have my books to turn to when my reserves weaken gives me strength. This combination empowers me. Turning to books is most certainly not conventional, nor recommended but for me a short-term resolution during a crisis.

I'm never seeking sympathy for what I experience, instead understanding of what triggers my symptoms and why what might seem unrelated actions might cause me an issue. However hard I work each day in order that I can live my best life, it can be destroyed in an instant if I'm not listened to—and heard—and it can be heart breaking when these simple things don't hit the radar of others.

Stepping beyond the front door, even during times of hypervigilance, is a calmer experience than during the first experience of

PTSD. During times of clarity, I can even class socialising as pleasurable. I'd never allow myself to become housebound or to get into the 'state' I was in whilst recovering from the assault again—but for anyone with PTSD it is an easy void to cascade into. Through pushing oneself beyond comfort zones my new normal means I'm not consumed by fear, anxiety nor indeed distracted in the constant combat of fighting PTSD. Having the freedom and ability to step over the threshold without thinking about the difficulties I might face is a relief difficult to place into words. Freedom, I guess, doesn't quite cover it. Liberty of the mind goes a small way towards expressing the relief my PTSD symptoms remain bubbling below the surface, rather than erupting like a volcano.

Quality of life is what makes the difference for me, in noticing a downward trend in my mental health and not ignoring it in order that a little discomfort in therapy doesn't manifest into anything more sinister.

This way healing occurs, and life can be decent again.

Chapter Thirty-Six

Final Word

Overcoming adversity, fear, PTSD—however I might choose to phrase what I've experienced—has most certainly been a hellish ride. Despite both the physical and psychological pain, I'd not be the person my lived experiences have shaped me into, nor would I have met so many incredible friends along the way. Ironically, the people I now know as a result of trauma—because of the experiences that life has placed before me (including the ones I've not gone into detail about) wouldn't have allowed these scary events to have continued. I know many people who would have removed me from the situation.

Without doubt, a triage of change in the way I look physically, perceive my personality and in physical strength are all aspects to have overcome and accept. In doing so I believe moving forward has become possible in conjunction with all the rest I've had to accept and achieve. There are hundreds of hurdles placed upon my path still proving my journey a tremendous battle. A battle I'll not give up on, one that is far from elegant, is most definitely unfiltered in respect of my response to situations, and one that frustrates as well as highly rewards.

Unfortunately, life has proven that symptoms of my complex disorders will, at times, threaten to overcome my psyche. I've proven to myself time and again that each occurrence of illness means I'm provided with an opportunity to bounce back stronger, and I know in my heart I'll continue to do so. This is testament not only to my desire to strive but also in finally feeling safe within my life (mostly). For the first time since adulthood there's a sense of inner security that holds me together which I'm able to draw upon ninety percent of the time. The bond I spoke about (the unconditional love that knows no boundaries) means I can finally feel as whole as I'll ever be and have ever been. That feeling of hunger; the hole that was left from being raped, is the smallest I've known it since that fateful day in two-thousand-and-three. Even during my times of crisis, when depression or PTSD strikes, I feel safe in Dave's arms (and I didn't ever think I'd say that of anyone).

With or without intervention of therapy and with my extensive knowledge of brain and body functions (as well as being therapeutically aware due to being qualified in the field) I can and will help myself. I've learnt to know what each chemical release feels like and know there's control over my adrenaline release. As a result, my body is beginning to repair. I'm under no illusion my body requires considerable time to recover from the years of adrenaline it has coped with but am thankful that it hasn't ended in a stroke or heart attack.

Being thrown in at the deep end; the very notion that all sense of stability or rational state had vanished, presented me with an extraordinary scenario that was threatening plunge me deeper into despair with each new therapeutic session. Despite not being able to see my way through the darkness, I didn't lose faith in my own ability to fight. Hope over adversity, however shallow that hope felt at times due to it being deeply hidden under layers of despair and depression, never left me. My desire for this book is that it conveys a strong message of hope to anyone facing the same issues or who is witnessing someone battling any of the symptoms discussed.

Giving up has never been and will never be my option.

Fear, if used correctly can be a powerful tool as I have shared. You only need to look towards politics or the mass media to view it working in the most powerful form (either positively or negatively). Obviously during domestic abuse and rape trauma cases fear is used negatively and in order to control and overpower. Others seeking power and control over another, do so in order to diminish their target's sense of being through grinding down their sense of worth to the point they are under complete control. This is how abusers use fear as it places them in strong manipulative positions—once I was in this position it took a long time to first realise it and then to escape from it. I'll not be in this position again nor will I allow anyone in my family to endure such abuse.

On the flipside—of the power I now hold over fear—I not only use the emotion in order to gain strength when I need it most, in order to fuel any battle that I'm required to overcome, but in order to defy it. In a book I've just discovered by Lord Moran, who was Sir Winston Churchill's personal doctor, "The Anatomy of Courage" (1945) speaks of how "imagination helps some men and destroys others". I can confirm that my most devastating times stem from the months I cannot write my fiction, so make of this what you will—but I'll save you the analysis and share that writing is my best therapy. It always will be.

In matter-of-factly speaking out about why my life led me down such a self-destructive path and how I gained strength from that in the end has bought me the clarity I so clearly needed. Let's face the facts. Eighty miles of road running was my self-harm and I'd not realised that until authoring this book. I've already stated it didn't allow me to escape my reality and so I sought other adrenaline fuelling sport. Not once had I or would I consider cutting myself, instead my body endured physical exercise until exhaustion hit. With my whole being PTSD overcame me due to my physical disability taking over and my inability not allowing this exercise routine to continue for I had too much thinking time on my hands! Now that it has captured my mind, it will always be something to live with and control.

With regards to evidence for this book, there are numerous emails, photographs, and letters I've kept. This includes an email stating how much I enjoyed being raped. Correspondence that was supposed to intimidate—to create fear—that now empowers me to have the courage to speak out. Although I've not disclosed all the events of the stalking years, and there's good reason for this, for my children only know the truth as far as the content of this book.

My closure came during a civil court case during which I represented myself. This gave me scope to push the boundaries as to the main reason behind why he and I were attending and got myself heard by the judge. With the new anti-stalking laws in place the same day I pushed hard against a family who had given me hell for so long. I was in court alone, unrepresented against the man who sat with his solicitor and overcame all those years of fear. I'd spoken about a lady by the name of Laura Richards and of Paladin, of the Suzy Lamplugh Trust and the work they do to CAFCAS and filled out a DASH form for them. I referenced evidence I had in a folder, that his solicitor had seen that morning. Despite having had my case heard at a Multi-Agency Risk Assessment Conference I was unaware of the result until the need of collecting my medical records after the assault causing brain trauma. It explained why, after the event, the police suddenly cared about my safety and wellbeing and were finally present for the last 'event,' a sickening phone call that came in on my landline. I answered, heard who it was and passed the phone over. The heavy breathing and panting continued but in their ears. The number wasn't withheld.

The result of the conference was that I was "at risk of serious harm or death." I'll let that hang in the air a moment.

Although it had felt tremendously grand to have finally been heard in court, it took a long time to stop looking over my shoulder—and despite this all happening inside a court room, there can never be a prosecution as part of the new law states that stalking and harassment preceding the said law coming into effect doesn't count. That's a kick in the teeth given it was far more than what I've shared in this book.

Fear, then, in circumstances such as post-trauma, that you can turn into power can be, as we have discovered, a powerful tool in overcoming your adversity. Used correctly fear is an all-important emotion that will take you far in your endeavours to regain a sense of self-worth. In owning your story and truly looking deep within yourself it's a fulfilling way to own who you are rather than being defined by what happened in your past. Through forward thinking you are able to carve out a positive future rather than to be trapped in a cycle of negativity—that's owning your story. Instead of using up your quota of courage, its forging new courage.

Embarking on psychological and criminological qualifications was, therapeutically, my way forward in the beginning. The so called 'after care' that happened after the stalking event, I found a personal insult. One that left me no room to breathe in a different form. It was too little far too late. Despite this, I was now building a picture on why people change—the grass roots of existence and of human behaviour. Each course within my studies led to another and within six months I'd authored essays on the subject I'd specialise in, in preparation for my PhD (that brain trauma prevented me from undertaking). These essays now form part of my thrillers.

Closure for me has come in the form of forgiveness for rape, forgiveness for stalking and forgiveness for the head injury. Each of these major events and the people involved have their freedom because of flaws in the law or lack of capacity. Is it any wonder I've fought so diligently against adrenaline and the other chemicals in my body? Now I've moved to a new county there might be a possibility to learn how to relax after all these years.

Perhaps not.

Regret isn't something I dwell upon. I could easily have continued my successful career in photography which was something I enjoyed immensely. Instead, I chose to work one to one with some of our most severely mentally damaged individuals, people who will never be able to live independently and who live behind locked doors and gates. Capacity is a difficult subject, knowing you shouldn't hit women and beating one up during psychosis when you're not capable of self-care or making your own breakfast tells me the person who changed my life wasn't responsible for their actions. It comes down to risk, to assessment and to those factors going very wrong at a time routines should have been perfected. When systems fail in extreme circumstances (and especially when they've not been fixed in weeks) in combination with complacency, the consequences can be terrifyingly catastrophic. I'm living proof that Health and Safety shouldn't be ignored, and that Risk Assessments are to be updated.

Let's look at the positives here. In surviving the attack at work, it placed perception on what I was designed to overcome. Feeling there was no alternative than to immediately forgive my attacker, which has got me thinking in more recent times. With all my heart, survival of my attack happened because I'd been toughened up as a result of the other two serious traumas—because the extreme brutality that had entered my life hardened me. That most definitely doesn't make any of that right. In point of fact I remember, during my interview, saying to my future boss that, "there's nothing the people here can throw in my direction that will shock me." That statement is true, they didn't shock despite all they threw in my direction or towards others. That said, some of their actions disappointed and appalled me. They never shocked me though.

Should this mean I'm thankful for my acquired brain injury? No, most certainly not but in order my life can move forward, I had to forgive everyone—and I have. Forgiveness was one of the more difficult processes to comprehend. In doing so it has allowed me to forge myself a new pathway. By stepping outside the negative cycle of destruction that had affected my life for a considerable number of years it allowed me to heal. I've healed from rape, from stalking and from brain trauma.

I'll never, ever forget though.

Spending the last year analysing my life in order to share it so openly to give insight into PTSD has meant taking a deep breath and considering the consequences for me. My utmost privacy in print. No turning back. I'm glad of it.

Freedom

Freedom of the mind, from the darkness within,
A willingness to allow my new life to begin.
Remembering suddenly easy, and stress free
My future looking bright I suddenly foresee.

Acceptance of the pain I live with, has to be,
Just every inch a part of me.
That all I've endured just adds to the depth,
Of all the shades that give me breadth.

The ability to let go, to finally see,
That what I've experienced has madeth me.
That who I was, and what happened before,
Shaped who I became so I dwell no more.

Happiness and well-being, so important to me,
To letting go of what used to be.
And embracing all the new-born ability,
Freedom of the mind and capability.

About the Author

Thank you for your interest in my writing.

Within my novels I encompass my knowledge of criminology and psychology. My characters are often corrupt with the intention of dragging others along with them. The storylines convey real life situations with dramatic consequences and race against the clock demands on life. Pushing boundaries of what might make you uncomfortable to read, rest assured it made me uncomfortable to write; but I never go beyond reality. My writing is dark, brutal, and often crawl, but there is a softer side, too.

As an advocate for mental health and, having survived trauma, I've written intensively about my own recovery on subjects close to my heart. Trauma is, after all, the reason I began writing.

I highlight my journalism on my Soul2Ink blog attached to my website.

For more information on my work, please visit, www.donnasiggers.com

Social media:
Facebook: https://www.facebook.com/donna.siggers
FB page: https://www.facebook.com/DonnaSiggersWrites
Twitter X: https://twitter.com/DonnaSiggers1
Instagram: https://instagram.com/donnasiggers72

TicTok: https://tictoc.com/donnasiggers
LinkedIn: https://www.linkedin.com/in/donnasiggers
Threads: https://www.threads.com/donnasiggers72

Printed in Great Britain
by Amazon

48826439R00106